Making Strategy Work

Building Sustainable Growth Capability

Timothy J. Galpin

Foreword by Walter R. Young

Jossey-Bass Publishers • San Francisco

Copyright © 1997 by Jossey-Bass Inc., Publishers, 350 Sansome Street,
San Francisco, California 94104.

Substantial discounts on bulk quantities of Jossey-Bass books are
available to corporations, professional associations, and other
organizations. For details and discount information, contact the
special sales department at Jossey-Bass Inc., Publishers
(415) 433-1740; Fax (800) 605-2665.

For sales outside the United States, please contact your local Simon &
Schuster International Office.

Jossey-Bass Web address: http://www.josseybass.com

Manufactured in the United States of America on Lyons Falls
TCF   Turin Book. This paper is acid-free and 100 percent totally
chlorine-free.

Library of Congress Cataloging-in-Publication Data

Galpin, Timothy J.
    Making strategy work : building sustainable growth capability /
Timothy J. Galpin.
        p.   cm. — (Jossey-Bass business & management series)
    Includes bibliographical references and index.
    ISBN 0-7879-1001-5 (alk. paper)
    1. Employee motivation.   2. Strategic planning.   3. Leadership.
4. Organizational change.   I. Title.   II. Series.
HF5549.5.M63G35   1997
658.4'012—dc21   97-24231

FIRST EDITION
HB Printing   10 9 8 7 6 5 4 3 2 1
JK

The Jossey-Bass

Business & Management Series

Contents

*To my father, Albert George Galpin, a true craftsman who
has made a lasting impression through his frequently used phrase,
"If you are going to do a job, do it right."*

Foreword

In *Making Strategy Work*, Timothy Galpin points out that even the best-planned strategies don't instantly turn into tangible results. If they did, all companies and their shareholders would be forever blissful, not to mention wealthy. Galpin demonstrates that the bridge between a company's strategy and its success is its people—the management and employees of the organization. Until a company's growth strategy (whether acquisition, internal growth, new market penetration, new products, or the like) and the people within the organization (their skills, competencies, and behaviors) are aligned, no plan will ever be fully realized.

Galpin describes and illustrates an approach to ensuring that people are focused on achieving the strategy of the organization—whatever the aims of that strategy may be. He provides a good overview of the strategy-setting process, leading to the most important aspect of any strategic effort: implementation. Following Galpin's advice will facilitate the success of organizations that are striving to transform their corporate plans into tangible results.

An illustration of the effectiveness of the approach that Galpin professes is the overwhelming success of Champion Enterprises, a producer of manufactured homes. To say the least, manufactured housing is not a glamour industry of the nineties, but at Champion Enterprises, our focus on profitable growth has enabled us to build a company whose stock has performed more like a high-tech company than one that uses chassis and wheels to build homes. Since coming to Champion as CEO in May of 1990, when the top executives were filling out papers for Chapter 11, I have seen sales rise from $311 million to approximately $2 billion in 1996, and operating losses turn around to double-digit annual earnings growth. Our market share has grown from about 4 percent to more than 17 percent in five years (making us the second-largest manufactured home producer), and Champion's stock price has risen about fortyfold over the past seven years. *Fortune* magazine selected Champion as one of the fastest growing companies in America in its October 14, 1996, issue, and *Forbes* singled us out as the company with the highest average return on equity in the construction industry, a result we accomplished with no debt.

The achievements recently enjoyed at Champion have not come easily in an industry traditionally characterized by fragmentation and plagued by a "not in my backyard" image. Our overriding formula for a successful strategy of profitable growth is simple: *focus, focus, focus.* For example, our focus on financial results has been providing shareholder value through a compounded earnings per share growth goal of more than 20 percent per year for three years. To accomplish this, we continue to need people whose core competencies include market innovation, change-readiness (we change whole plants over in a weekend and make distribution changes in less than sixty days), local accountability, and a "keep it simple" approach. To create these competencies at Champion we have incorporated many of the management systems, structure, operations, and incentives that Galpin identifies throughout *Making Strategy Work* as being key to aligning people with the aims of a given strategy.

For example, over the past several years we have been consolidating a fragmented industry by focusing on both internal growth and acquisitions. Whereas our competition is centralized and integrated, Champion is largely decentralized. We have thirty-four autonomous business units with fifty housing plants dispersed geographically throughout the United States. To make decentralization work, our structure includes a lean corporate staff of fifty—including secretaries—in rented offices. There are no corporate jets or lavish perks. We have focused goals at every level of the organization. In addition, executive pay is tied to performance, and Champion's eleven thousand employees are all on incentives. As we continue to redefine the housing industry (one-third of all homes in the United States are now manufactured), the continuing alignment of our people with the business strategy will, as *Making Strategy Work* demonstrates, be critical.

Tim Galpin's book is full of useful information and clear examples about the most difficult aspect of strategy: making it work. Galpin provides companies with a pragmatic approach to ensure that people are focused on achieving the business strategy, whatever its aims may be. Following his advice will facilitate the success of any organization striving to transform its growth strategy into tangible, bottom-line results.

Auburn Hills, Michigan   Walter R. Young
August 1997

Preface

Strategic planning has returned to the forefront of competitive thought on shaping commerce into the next millennium. Yet many business leaders would argue that strategy never left the collective corporate consciousness. They would contend that the downsizing and cost cutting of the early 1990s were the strategies of choice for that time. This may be true; however, focusing activities on the cost side of the profit equation was a relatively simple strategy to pursue. With laptops in hand, armies of consultants were employed to churn out graphs, charts, and tables that bolstered recommended head-count reductions in organizations across the globe. These activities are now giving way to more popular growth activities. Strategies such as mergers and acquisitions, new market penetration, mass customization, enhanced customer service, strategic alliances, and the like are all in the sights of businesses large and small. But management is quickly learning that developing a growth strategy, although a difficult exercise, is not nearly as exhausting as implementing it.

Unfortunately, the traditional strategy implementation scenario follows an all too familiar pattern that goes much like this: First, there is often surprise that planning is even taking place. Consultants are brought in by senior management. They set up in a back room somewhere with a small team of management and employees (included for "involvement purposes"). The strategists come out after several months with the "golden answer" neatly bound in a four-inch binder, complete with supporting data and documentation. Then comes some "communication" about the new strategic plan from the CEO or president (usually a written announcement and some management meetings that "cascade" through the organization). Next there is interpretation. What does the new strategy mean in terms of action I can take? is a question often heard in corporate hallways. Managers come away from announcement meetings wondering what the strategy really means to them and their people, and they fill in the blanks with their own explanations and actions. Finally, some managers take action and some do not. These steps add up to an elegant planning exercise followed by poor implementation. In fact, even *Consultants News,* a publication focused on the state and direction of the consulting industry, recently asserted that the "death knell for traditional strategy firms is clearly overstated. But it's apparent that McKinsey, BCG, Bain, et al. can't keep ignoring implementation to sustain growth" ("Continued Growth—But. . .," p. 4). Planning that is done with disregard for the need to align people with the strategy creates, at the least, disinterest among employees and management when new strategies are announced, and at the worst, distrust and contempt for new strategies that people either do not want to implement or believe they do not have the necessary skills to achieve. Clearly there is a need for better approaches to making strategy work.

There *is* a better way. Through trial and error, management is now realizing that the only way to implement strategies effectively is through people. But getting people to act on a chosen strategy has been elusive. For years companies have tried various implementation approaches, including presenting employees with airtight analytics that back up management's strategic rationale, selling people on the merits of the strategy, issuing edicts about implementation requirements, and making grand announcements via large rallies. These management actions only begin to scratch the surface of strategy implementation. What really makes the difference between successful and unsuccessful strategy implementation is the way management motivates and educates people to act on a new strategy.

Purpose and Audience

Making Strategy Work was conceived as both a foundational text and a pragmatic how-to handbook to help both line and support-function management (human resources, systems, finance, and so on) implement their strategies faster, more efficiently, and more effectively. The book clearly illustrates the underpinnings of strategic planning, presents a model for making strategy work through the *human assets* within an organization, provides research and case examples of real companies' strategy implementation successes, and demonstrates the application of a focused project perspective to achieve more effective and efficient strategy implementation. Because strategies can be organization-wide, divisional, or even departmental in scope, this book can be used by senior executives for organization-wide strategy implementation as well as by middle management and supervisors for suborganizational strategy implementation in their divisions or departments, in both line and support functions.

Throughout the text are many examples of companies and their strategies, implementation approaches, and relative accomplishments. In corporations as in any other learning situation, information, innovation, and understanding progress continuously. Consequently, the examples included are time-based. Today's successful companies become the dinosaurs of tomorrow if they are unable to make their strategies work. Likewise, the laggards of today can become the leaders of tomorrow. The reader should view the examples as illustrative of the points being made and not as timeless gospel of the business world. Such a gospel does not exist, especially in today's rapidly changing global environment.

Overview of the Contents

Making Strategy Work is separated into two main parts. Part One presents a synopsis of strategic planning and an approach to successful strategy implementation. Chapter One provides the reader with an overview of strategic planning—its roots, evolution, and application—and the Making Strategy Work Model, on which the contents of the text are based. A pictorial view of the model is presented along with an explanation of the logic behind it. Chapter Two identifies the common patterns and the results achieved in successful strategy implementation efforts.

The chapters in Part Two present a pragmatic, how-to approach to strategy implementation. Chapter Three discusses how to establish a dedicated project approach to effectively coordinate and progress an organization's strategy implementation efforts. The chapter identifies clear project roles, accountabilities, structure, time lines, and milestones that when applied successfully expedite strategy implementation. Chapters Four through Nine detail the steps in the Making Strategy Work Model. Each chapter builds on the contents of earlier chapters, using templates, charts, graphs, and tools to illustrate the activities and techniques that go into executing well-coordinated strategy implementation. Finally, Chapter Ten presents a project "road map" that summarizes the pragmatic steps of effective strategy implementation. The chapter also identifies the common mistakes management commits when attempting to make strategies work, and the factors that lead to success.

In addition to these chapters, the book contains four appendixes. Appendixes A, B, and C are guidebooks for the various teams typically involved in the project structure of a well-coordinated strategy implementation effort, and Appendix D contains a table that summarizes the current strategy implementation research discussed in Chapter Two. Finally, definitions of key terms are provided in the glossary.

Until now, no text had effectively *operationalized* strategy implementation; there existed no comprehensive how-to book that presented a clear pragmatic approach. The chapters of *Making Strategy Work* provide readers with examples, research, and a pragmatic, proven approach to designing, implementing, and tracking substantive strategic, growth-oriented change within an organization—strategic change that not only can be managed, but that also can produce measurable results.

Acknowledgments

Few if any works ever represent the knowledge of only one person. This text is no exception. It reflects concepts, insights, and experiences garnered from numerous people within industry and consulting alike, both domestically and internationally. Colleagues, clients, friends, and family all have provided their input in some way. I cannot include all the names of these "contributors" here, but specifically I would like to thank Donald Robinson, Robert Gilbreath, Michael PreFontaine, Robert Corliss, Tania Modic, Midge Rothrock, Patrick Murray, and John Hooper for their particular guidance on this topic. As for all of the others, I trust they will accept a simple thank you as an expression of my sincere gratitude and appreciation.

Dallas, Texas   Timothy J. Galpin
August 1997

The Author

TIMOTHY J. GALPIN is practice leader for Human Resources Strategy at Watson Wyatt Worldwide. He received his Ph.D. degree in organization development from the University of California, Los Angeles, and has extensive experience in industry and consulting in both North America and Europe. He has authored several articles dealing with strategic change, performance improvement, merger integration, and organizational productivity, which have appeared in such publications as *Journal of Business Strategy, HR Magazine, Training and Development Journal, Mergers & Acquisitions, Human Resource Professional,* and *Employment Relations Today.* His first book is *The Human Side of Change* (1996), also published by Jossey-Bass.

Part One

From Strategic Planning to Sustainable Growth

The Making Strategy Work Model

Chapter One

Strategy

Easier Set Than Done

Even though its existence has been relatively brief (see Figure 1.1), strategic planning has made an impact on commerce like no other "movement" has. Since its conception in the early 1960s, when two Harvard professors—Ken Andrews and C. Roland Christensen—described the process, strategic planning has been applied by organizations large and small to shape their futures.

During the early 1960s, management viewed organizations as sets of individual functions (that is, marketing, production, finance, personnel, and so forth). Andrews and Christensen characterized the notion of strategy as a way to view organizations holistically (Byrne, 1996). Their depiction of organizations provided management with a means of determining a company's strengths and weaknesses relative to its competition. Thus began the formalized competitive analysis approach to strategy that is still popular today throughout the corporate world. Companies such as General Electric and the auto producers began to build centralized staffs of forward-thinking strategic planners, who were given the task of examining the position of products in the marketplace relative to competitors.

Throughout the remainder of the 1960s and the 1970s, strategic consulting "boutiques" were born. These firms came equipped with numerous planning models and tools to ensure that no stone was left unturned in the planning process. Macroeconomic and societal trends, political and regulatory shifts, technological developments, and competitor profiles, among other elements, were all factored into detailed planning analyses. In 1980, Michael Porter authored the planning text entitled *Competitive Strategy: Techniques*

Figure 1.1 History of Strategic Planning

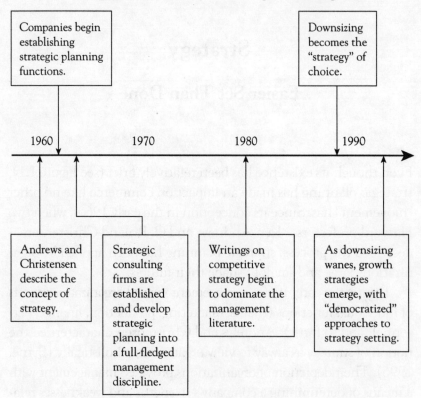

for Analyzing Industries and Competitors. His work supplemented the rigorous analytical techniques of the strategy firms by providing new planning models based on economic theories. Together they gave rise to the "science" of strategic planning.

In the late 1980s and the first half the 1990s, companies that had been beaten up by overseas competitors and more nimble start-up firms focused on extensive "reengineering" to increase the efficiency of their operations. Massive layoffs came from this wave of downsizing, leading to a short-term spike in profits but eventually resulting in a backlash of low morale and reduced commitment from employees and management.

Following the corporate thinning of the early 1990s, companies are now focusing on growth strategies. New planning gurus describe corporate futures based on *white space, coalitions, strategic intent, value migration, business ecosystems*, and *core competencies* (see the glossary for definitions of these terms). These new strategists have focused their efforts on the next wave of corporate growth: *creating new markets*, not just playing catch-up with competitors. As a result, companies are moving into new industries and building strength in areas previously overlooked by themselves and their competitors.

Strategic Trends

Since Andrews and Christensen described the concept of strategic planning, popular strategies have evolved from being clearly analytical exercises to being eclectic approaches that combine analytics with qualitative information (see Figure 1.2). For instance, during the 1970s productivity improvement was fashionable. This strategy entailed stopwatch-toting industrial engineers looking to eke the most they could out of streamlining tasks. The 1980s saw the rise of the Total Quality movement, led by people such as W. Edwards Deming and Phillip Crosby. Japanese companies paved the way for quality gains, and the rest of the world had to follow in order to compete. The early 1990s began the era of massive corporate downsizing, especially in the United States. Managing corporate profits became what Gary Hamel and C. K. Prahalad (1994) have called *denominator management*. They contend that "denominator management is an accountant's shortcut to asset productivity" (p. 9). The denominator is investment, and return on investment (or net income, the numerator, divided by investment) can be achieved in two basic ways—either by cutting the denominator (assets, headcount, and so forth) or by increasing the numerator. As the pressure from analysts and investors for short-term performance mounted, managers took the path of least resistance—they cut the denominator. True, during the 1980s many companies grew into huge bureaucracies, looking and, more important, performing more like governments than like businesses. And these bureaucracies began to weigh down companies

Figure 1.2 History of Strategic Trends

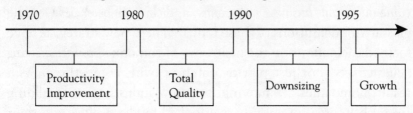

like huge anchors. They created an inward focus that caused customer service to grind to a screeching halt and resulted in skyrocketing costs along with sinking revenues, market share, and profits. Moreover, relatively simple decisions (such as whether to give a refund or whether a product should still be serviced under warranty) had to pass through multiple layers of management before being made. Company policy manuals began to look like multivolume encyclopedias. Downsizing streamlined much of the bureaucratic weight that companies were carrying. However, it did not cure all ills. The spikes in profit from reduced costs through downsizing only lasted a short time. Eventually, companies had little room for personnel cutbacks. Likewise, the glorification of corporate slashers was short-lived. Initially praised for excising the fat that grew out of the corporate overindulgence of the 1980s, downsizers have recently become the demons of the business world. Numerous news articles have vilified the likes of "Chainsaw" Al Dunlap and his disciples. The need now is for companies to grow intelligently. As you will see later in this book, growth is a more difficult strategy to pursue than downsizing. It requires that people be engaged in the business rather than released from it. Even Michael Hammer, the management guru who began the reengineering craze that induced companies to issue thousands of pink slips during the early 1990s, is quoted in a recent *Wall Street Journal* article as saying the following about the impact of downsizing on people: "I wasn't smart enough about that. I was reflecting my engineering background and was insufficiently appreciative of the human dimension. I've learned that's critical" (White, 1996, p. 1).

In his 1979 *Harvard Business Review* article entitled "How Competitive Forces Shape Strategy," Porter's opening line is, "The essence of strategy formulation is coping with competition" (p. 137). Since then, many have shared Porter's view of *competitive strategy.* Staying ahead of the competition was, and often still is, seen as the driving force behind planning for a company's future. Vying for market share and customer base within industries has been the foundation of competitive advantage.

Porter (1979) identifies five basic forces that steer industry competition: (1) the threat of new entrants, (2) the bargaining power of customers, (3) the bargaining power of suppliers, (4) the threat of substitute products or services, and (5) jockeying for position among current industry competitors (for example, by making price adjustments, instituting advertising campaigns, and so forth). On the basis of Porter's analytical approach, managers for the first time had a systematic means of evaluating their competitive surroundings. Research findings support Porter's concept of the impact that industry forces have on company performance. In his examination of the causes of performance differences among companies, Richard Schmalensee (1985) found that industry performance is the greatest predictor of individual company performance. Likewise, Pankaj Ghemawat (1986) studied one hundred companies that outperformed their industry competitors. He contends that there are three basic categories of "sustainable advantages" that companies can possess that are tied to industry economics: (1) size in the market, (2) access to resources or customers, and (3) restrictions on competitors' options (such as patents, antitrust laws, and being locked into prior investments). Moreover, Cynthia Montgomery and Michael Porter (1991) assert, "Out of the work on industry analysis has come a body of research on positioning a firm within its industry. Any company's performance is partly a result of the structure of its industry. . . . Positioning a company in its industry is based on the search for competitive advantage" (p. xv). Finally, in his latest discourse, entitled "What Is Strategy?" Porter (1996) maintains that the recent move away from viewing strategy as market positioning is "dangerous." He continues to believe that strategy is, in essence, competitive, but he offers a revised interpretation. He asserts that "a company can outperform rivals only if it can establish a difference that it can preserve" (p. 62) and that "competitive strategy is about being different. It means deliberately choosing a different set of activities to deliver a unique mix of value" (p. 64).

Since Porter introduced the concept of competitive strategy a few decades ago, management has religiously pursued a competitive approach to strategy. Take, for example, the recent strategies developed by a large utility based in the Southwest and by a midsize oil and natural gas producer based in the Midwest. The companies' 1996 strategy documents clearly identify the focus of their planning processes. Both firms based their strategies on detailed analyses of macroeconomic trends, societal trends, political and regulatory trends, technology trends, and direct competitors. In fact, the two companies organized large sections of their strategy reports under these very headings.

Recently, the concept of becoming *different* rather than competitive has become the focus of many companies. This view was popularized by Hamel and Prahalad in their 1993 article entitled "Strategy as Stretch and Leverage," which describes their view of the difference between competitive strategy and strategy as "stretch." They argue that competitive analysis enables management only to understand what the competition is doing and what the realities of the present are, and to peer a short distance into the future. Moreover, the normal analyses of market conditions, macroeconomic conditions, competitive trends, and so on allow managers to externalize the reasons for a company's performance. Companies that continually depend on strategic approaches to industry competitiveness will inevitably always play catch-up. Even when a company moves past its competition, after a short time that competition will learn what to do to move out in front. It then becomes catch-up time again.

Whether called stretch, extension, reinvention, leap, reach, or something else, the strategic concept of moving a business into an uncharted future is unlike viewing strategy as competitiveness. Hamel and Prahalad (1994) pose several questions designed to differentiate the competitive strategists from those who take a distinct view of the future. For example, they ask managers to determine whether they are maintenance managers or architects of the future, whether their initiatives (such as cycle-time reduction, enhanced service, and quality) are creating new industry advantages or are just catch-up activities, and whether they are as enthusiastic about pursuing new business and growth as they are about obtaining operational efficiency and downsizing. The authors contend, "Our point is simple: It is not enough for a company to get smaller and better and faster, as important as these tasks may be; a company must also be capable of fundamentally reconceiving its industry. In short, a company must also be capable of getting different" (1994, p. 16).

Nicholas Imparato and Oren Harari, in *Jumping the Curve: Innovation and Strategic Choice in an Age of Transition* (1994), present the notion of strategy as a leap. The authors use a variation of the organizational life-cycle curve developed by Richard Foster and John Butler (see Figure 1.3) to illustrate their thesis. Although their concept is not new (the S-curve is now commonly used to describe organizational life cycles), Imparato and Harari contend that to succeed in the future, organizations must leave their original life cycle behind to pursue a new life cycle. They describe four organizing principles that a company can employ to move from being "stabilizing" to "innovating":

1. *Look a customer ahead.* Leave behind today's products and services to pursue tomorrow's opportunities.
2. *Build the company around the software and build the software around the customer.* Change a company's priorities from building mass and size to increasing organizational competence.
3. *Ensure that those who live the values and ideals of the organization are the most rewarded and the most satisfied.* Harness the collective talents of people with one cohesive set of values and priorities.

4. *Treat the customer as the final arbiter of service and product quality by offering an unconditional guarantee of complete satisfaction.* Develop both the structure and the culture to support an organization-wide responsibility to ensure that the customer will be completely satisfied after a sale is made (1994, pp. 75–77).

Clearly illustrating a "stretch strategy," CEO Jack Welch is pursuing a direction that will build General Electric's (GE) future in the services arena. A long-standing industrial icon, GE has not been without its ups and downs. When Welch took over in the early 1980s, he spent much of his energy getting the bloated giant back to productivity. He reduced payrolls, did away with old-line businesses, and vastly improved the company's manufacturing productivity. Now, building on the managerial strength that GE has developed since Welch's arrival, the company is packaging those attributes and selling them to others. GE is now helping power plants to work more efficiently, developing an electronic tracking system to manage railroad rolling stock, operating engine service shops for airlines, and even establishing and running computer networks for corporations that will compete with industry giants IBM and EDS.

Figure 1.3 Discontinuity of Organizational Life Cycles

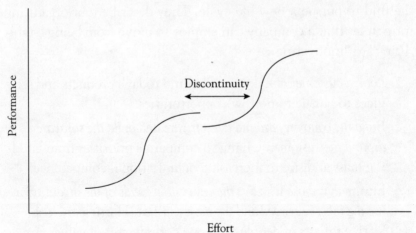

Source: Adapted from Foster, 1986, p. 102.

These service industries are nontraditional undertakings for a large manufacturing company such as GE. But they all build on what GE has learned from it's own internal efforts to become more managerially efficient, effective, and productive. GE's predicted change in revenue mix from 1995 to 2000 is to move from 43.5 percent manufacturing revenues to an estimated 33 percent, and from 50.5 percent services revenues (financial, aftermarket, and information services) to an estimated 62 percent (Smart, 1996).

Another company that is pursuing the "white space" outside its traditional industry is Tenneco. As part of reducing its operating costs under the leadership of CEO Dana Mead, the approximately $7 billion conglomerate has established a 225-employee shared service center in The Woodlands, Texas, called Tenneco Business Services (TBS). The center provides administrative services to Tenneco business units, ranging from taxes to payroll to information services and purchasing. By eliminating parallel pay systems and record keeping, and by consolidating local purchasing to get better deals, the new unit is expected to reduce costs enough to add an estimated 1.5 points to its operating margin. The company already believes that its service center is differentiated from those established by other companies, such as AlliedSignal and Baxter International, in that TBS supplies a wider range of services, including finance and accounting, human resources and payroll, employee benefits, data processing, environmental health and safety, and supplier relationship development (Plishner, 1996). But TBS is not just differentiated as a one-stop shopping service center or a successful cost-cutting exercise. The company has plans to turn the service center into a growth opportunity by marketing TBS's services to customers outside of Tenneco. The first will be the Newport News shipyard, which will become independent from Tenneco in 1997.

In addition to competitive approaches to strategy or strategy as stretch, the way to the future is sometimes through the past. Many companies were founded on the concept of customer service. However, with the rapid advancement of technology, a heavy focus on internal know-how, and large investments in research and development, firms find themselves internally focused, with little true interest in the customer. Going back to the customer as a source of strategic insight can be powerful. Kenichi Ohmae (1982, 1988) clearly makes a case for such a focus. He contends that the customer is actually the foundation of all strategy and that a company must consider and respond to customer needs as they shift over time. Moreover, Ohmae asserts that customers should take priority even over shareholders, because a company that consistently serves its customers better than its competitors will enjoy greater profitability. Ohmae states, "Looking closely at a customer's needs, thinking deeply about a product—these are no exotic pieces of strategic apparatus. They are, as they have always been, the basics of sound management. They have just been neglected or ignored" (1988, p. 73).

No better example of getting back to basics to regenerate successful growth is that of IBM's recent resurgence. At the time of this writing, IBM's revenue is on pace to grow 7 to 10 percent through 1997. Moreover, IBM's stock has risen from approximately $129 per share in October 1996 to more than $155 per share in November 1996, and analysts are predicting that it will reach $195 per share by the end of 1997 (Sager, 1996). What is the explanation for IBM's growth since the arrival of chairman and chief executive Louis Gerstner? *Back to basics.* Sager states, "The secret to IBM's success isn't great technology, cutthroat pricing, or flashy marketing moves. It's approaching double-digit growth for the first time in almost seven years for one main reason: Under Gerstner, IBM has gone back to the most basic notion of how to succeed in business: talking to customers, learning their needs, and figuring out how to satisfy them" (pp. 155–156).

The Impact of Strategy Setting on Implementation

The way a strategy is developed has an impact on the way it is implemented. When planning does not take into account the implications of aligning people with the strategy, the effort is doomed to failure.

A common approach to developing strategy is the *ivory tower exercise*. Early on, corporate strategies became the domain of a select group of senior management, the planning function, and consultants. In his discussion about the strategy setting of the mid–1960s, John Byrne (1996) states, "In its heyday, strategy-spinning was the ultimate left-brain exercise for the corporate elite. Thousands of B-school-trained thinkers sat high in the climate-controlled aeries of bloated business empires, crunching numbers and spinning scenarios to conquer adversaries. . . . Everything could be categorized, analyzed, quantified, and predicted. You could plot a strategy that would safely steer your company to uninterrupted triumph if only you *thought* hard enough" (p. 46). This view is indicative of the elitist approach to strategy development that not only was used in the sixties but that also is not uncommon today. Management is now realizing, however, that strategy setting by the elite has not produced and continues not to produce the results they need. They are finding that what looks good to the best educated business minds does not always work in reality and is often too complex or heady for the people who really need to understand it in order to implement it—the company's management and employees.

Many companies are now employing a more *democratized* approach to setting strategy, involving greater numbers of people throughout the organization. Teams of line and staff personnel are being engaged in the process. Often junior employees are involved to make use of their creative thinking ability, because they are not yet wearing the corporate blinders that many long-serving people do. Additionally, older management (those near retirement) are selected for their ability to "tell it like it is." Moreover, keeping planning near the realities of the marketplace often compels companies to involve customers and suppliers in the strategy-setting process (Byrne, 1996), a practice that is in direct conflict with the old notions of strategic planning, which has traditionally been one of the most clandestine of corporate activities.

In their groundbreaking discussion of strategy, Hamel and Prahalad (1994) promote an approach to strategy development that includes people from across intracompany boundaries. They contend that this horizontal inclusion in the strategy setting process addresses interlinkages in organizations that are critical to collective action. "What we argue for . . . is not absolute decentralization, nor a heavy-handed *corporate* strategy, but what might be described as enlightened *collective* strategy. . . . The development of collective strategy requires managers to adopt a more cooperative and less competitive posture vis-à-vis their peers. They must recognize that for every instance of resource sharing, cross-unit support, or sacrifice for the greater good, there may not be an immediate *quid pro quo*" (p. 318). Henry Mintzberg (1994) describes a process by which planners are data suppliers to management rather than strategy setters themselves. He contends that managers, using a combination of data and "soft" insights (such as personal experiences), are the real strategists within organizations. He comments, "Strategic planning often spoils strategic thinking, causing managers to confuse real vision with the manipulation of numbers. . . . The most successful strategies are visions, not plans" (p. 107).

In addition to the views of strategy-setting gurus like Hamel, Prahalad, and Mintzberg, consider the following examples, which illustrate involvement-oriented approaches to strategy development that set the stage for effective implementation:

- At Hewlett-Packard (HP), Chairman Lewis Platt sees his most important role as building bridges between the various operational units of the company. Platt states, "I don't create business strategies. . . . My role is to encourage discussion of the white spaces, the overlap and gaps among business strategies, the important areas that are not addressed by the strategies of individual HP businesses" (Byrne, 1996, p. 50). HP regularly holds sessions on the "business ecosystem" that include managers from various manufacturing units, as well as customers and suppliers. By involving these nontraditional participants in discussion about the state of the company and the industry, management gains critical views of the potential marketplace that they would not normally see.

- In a slow-growth, mature market, J. M. Smucker Company, an Ohio-based maker of jams and jellies, put a team of 140 employees (approximately 7 percent of its workforce) to work on a major new strategy for the company. They devoted 50 percent of their work time for six months to the project. Twelve initiatives came out of the exercise that the company believes could double its current sales of $635 million over the next five years. For instance, the company has entered into an alliance with Brach & Brock Confections to produce Smucker's jellybeans—the beginning of several co-branded products. The idea for the co-branding arrangement was generated by staff who would not have had a role in a normal strategy-setting exercise. President Richard K. Smucker says of the endeavor, "Instead of having just 12 minds working it, we really used the 140 as ambassadors to solicit input from all 2,000 employees. . . . It gave us a broader perspective, and it brought to the surface a lot of people with special talents" (Byrne, 1996, p. 52).

Traditional Implementation Approaches Do Not Work

Growth strategies are more difficult to develop and document than downsizing, and once contrived, they present management with an even greater challenge—how to make them work. Turning strategic plans into tangible business results can frustrate even the most experienced manager. Once a company has determined its strategy, whether competitive, stretch, back to basics, or a combination of these, the next and most monumental task is to bring the strategy to fruition.

Traditional approaches to strategy implementation fail for several reasons. First, implementation is usually an afterthought of the process. Although the democratized approach to strategy setting described earlier helps to facilitate deployment (because more than just a select few have been involved), implementation implications are often overlooked during strategy development. Second, once strategies are set, management usually falls back on rudimentary implementation activities, such as issuing a memo from the president, gathering a large group of employees at the head office, requiring employees to attend a new training course, or distributing newly minted binders containing the details of the strategy. Third, implementation activities usually occur only during the first few months following the finalization of the strategy and are scarce thereafter. Little management effort to make the new strategy a reality is put forth for any extended period. Finally, management often lacks the willingness, ability, and long-term commitment to leverage the organization's strategic resources—capital or human—to make the strategy work.

The Making Strategy Work Model

What is the key to successful strategy implementation? Realigning an organization's "influence systems" in order to change individual and organizational behaviors—a process I have called the Making Strategy Work Model, illustrated in Figure 1.4.

Influence Systems

In the past, management has tried to *control* people's actions through stringent rules and policies or by issuing edicts, but even though some employees respond to this approach, in general management has met with little success. The reality is that people are not actually under anyone's direct control. They are only *influenced* by the makeup of their work environment.

For example, in the military, when a sergeant tells a group of privates to "paint that fence," the privates usually respond quickly by painting the fence. Some would call that control. However, upon taking a closer look it is obvious that the privates are responding to their organizational environment. For instance, soldiers have rules clearly communicated to them; the negative consequences of not painting the fence are understood, and the positive consequences—if they paint enough fences and paint them well— are also clear (for example, promotion to the next rank). They also receive training, rewards and recognition, and so on. So, even though control appears to exist, people *in all organizations*, large,

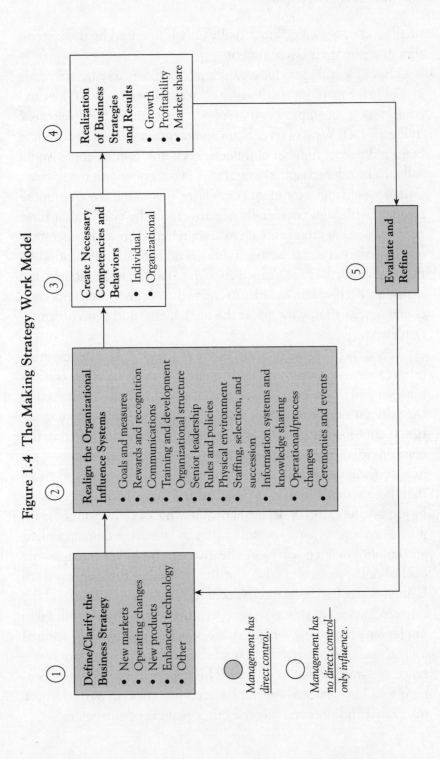

Figure 1.4 The Making Strategy Work Model

① Define/Clarify the Business Strategy

- New markets
- Operating changes
- New products
- Enhanced technology
- Other

② Realign the Organizational Influence Systems

- Goals and measures
- Rewards and recognition
- Communications
- Training and development
- Organizational structure
- Senior leadership
- Rules and policies
- Physical environment
- Staffing, selection, and succession
- Information systems and knowledge sharing
- Operational/process changes
- Ceremonies and events

③ Create Necessary Competencies and Behaviors

- Individual
- Organizational

④ Realization of Business Strategies and Results

- Growth
- Profitability
- Market share

⑤ Evaluate and Refine

Management has __direct control.__

Management has __no direct control—__ only influence.

small, and in-between, are actually only influenced by the systems that make up their environment.

I have identified twelve organizational influence systems that are available for management to use to create necessary behaviors and competencies in employees that support the business plan (see box 2 in Figure 1.4). Why twelve? Solid arguments can be made for there being a different number of influence systems. Some people would call for a broader grouping of five or six major organizational systems. Others would argue for more granularity, suggesting fifteen or more systems. Although potentially controversial, the twelve that have been chosen are broad enough to comprehensively address strategy implementation across various industries and organizational sizes. At the same time, they are focused enough to facilitate redesigning and managing each system in order to create the necessary behaviors and competencies that will support the implementation of an organization's strategy.

Who "owns" these systems? None of them is the sole responsibility of any one person or department, although in many companies, several of the twelve systems have traditionally been seen as the purview of one function, such as human resources or information technology, or of a department within a function, such as the compensation or training departments within human resources. Yet many organizations have learned through numerous trials and errors that these systems cannot be designed and implemented effectively by just one function or department. Viewing and addressing the influence systems as *jointly owned* by line and functional management and employees is a much more effective approach. For example, the traditional approach at a large utility located in the southwestern United States had been to view communications, training, and the other influence systems as separate entities. Yet as they mobilized to implement their new service strategy management, they formed joint teams of representatives from the line, from information systems, and from human resources. This approach enabled the company to address its strategy implementation effort in a much more integrated and systemic way than they had ever done before.

The Logic Behind the Model

The Making Strategy Work Model is based on collective management thought about corporate strategy that is just now arriving at some important conclusions. First, design and planning is only the beginning, *not* the deliverable. Successful implementation leading to tangible business results (such as revenue growth, increased market share, and enhanced profitability) is the desired outcome. Second, people are the key bridge between an organization's strategy and its business results. They choose either to change or not to change what they do in order to implement a strategy as planned. Third, management does not have direct control over people's actions; they only have influence. Management does, however, have direct control over the content of business plans and strategies, and over the organizational systems that influence people's behaviors. Fourth, telling people to change what they do is not enough. Communication is only one of the twelve organizational influence systems, and communicating something new without realigning the other influence systems with the new strategy only confuses people and continues to reinforce the old strategy. Fifth, the organizational influence systems are systemic in that they interact with one another to create individual and organizational behaviors. That is, you can't just change one and leave the others alone. Finally, management cannot wait until the planning process is complete to begin implementation. They should begin with the planning process itself. As noted earlier, many companies have found that the "closed door" approach to planning makes for poor implementation, and as a result, planning is being pushed down to the users. Early in his tenure, Jack Welch dismantled GE's planning function and placed the planning process in the hands of management and employees— those who must implement. Doing this begins to build grassroots knowledge and understanding, and enables all employees to buy into the business strategy.

The underlying premise of the Making Strategy Work Model (Figure 1.4), then, is that *there is a critical relationship between aligning an organization's influence systems and creating necessary behaviors and competencies in order to achieve desired business results.* Although management has direct control over the contents of the business strategy (box 1), it does not have direct control over the realization of that strategy and its desired results (box 4). Senior and mid-level management, supervisors, and employees are the key bridge between the business strategy and tangible results; people *at all organizational levels* must act on implementing the strategy through the competencies they possess and the behaviors they exhibit (box 3). Management does not have direct control over people's behaviors or competencies; people must be given incentives to implement the strategy or their part of it. Beyond revised pay programs (although they are an important driving force), incentives take the form of the twelve influence systems (box 2). Management has direct control over the form taken by each of these systems. Finally, motivating management and employee behavior and competencies through the twelve influence systems leads to strategy implementation and measurable desired business results.

Although the Making Strategy Work Model can be used to facilitate reengineering, technology implementation, and the like, it is fundamentally a growth model. By way of contrast, Figure 1.5 illustrates a cost-cutting/downsizing strategy implementation model. The only component of realizing a company's business strategy and gaining desired results that management has at least some direct control over is cost cutting. Management can downsize a workforce by 10 percent, 20 percent, 30 percent, or more, and these savings drop directly to the bottom line. That is why investment analysts maintain such a preference for companies that announce downsizing plans. In this model, the logic goes immediately from management having direct control over the contents of the business strategy (cost cutting through downsizing, box 1) to the realization of the strategy and desired results (cost savings and increased operating profit, box 2). This model literally removes the bridge of people, and often the need for coordinated management of the twelve influence systems. But to "grow" a company, including creating new

Figure 1.5 Cost-Cutting/Downsizing Strategy Implementation Model

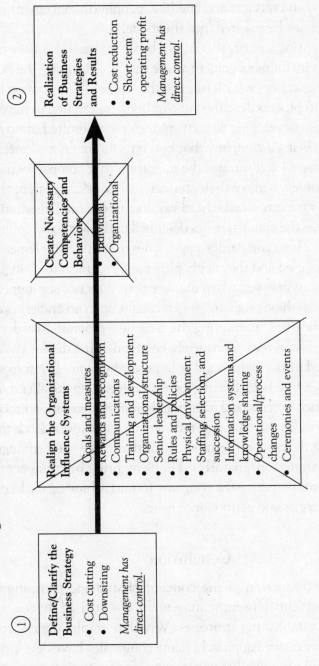

markets and products; making operating changes; enhancing marketing, sales, and service; and the like, people (management and employees) must be inserted into the model.

Implementing strategy should not be viewed as a side issue or a parallel activity for management while they are "running the business." Making strategy work *is* running the business. The strategy implementation process described in this book is designed to move a company from developing elegant strategies with limited or no deployment to being a company that builds its future on *implemented strategies*. Figure 1.6 illustrates the migration that companies must undergo in order to make their strategies work. Management that wonders why it cannot make headway on strategy implementation often possesses the characteristics described in the left-hand column of the figure. These companies' approaches to strategy implementation are unfocused and they apply piecemeal programs to changing the company. Worse yet, when management does not see immediate results from these programs, it gets caught up in an endless cycle of shifting priorities, attempting the next new program in order to get an immediate return. Conversely, companies that display the attributes listed in the right-hand column of the figure begin to see their strategies take hold. Staying focused, integrating the alignment of key influence systems, and adjusting their implementation process on the basis of clear performance measures creates the dividends that management desires. Furthermore, firms that make their strategies work concentrate continuously on implementing high-impact influence systems that drive the company toward achieving its desired business strategies and performance goals.

Conclusion

Since the introduction of the concept of strategic planning by Andrews and Christensen, management has utilized diverse approaches to establishing strategies. Whether employing an *ivory tower* or a *democratized* approach, many companies have developed numerous and often well-thought-out plans for their futures. Yet

Figure 1.6 Company Migration to Making Strategies Work

From	To
Planning separated from implementation	Planning and implementation interwoven
Organizational influence systems characterized by unrelated programs and interventions	Organizational influence systems that are integrated
Short-term adjustments to the influence systems	Long-term alignment of key influence systems with the business strategy
Unfocused, constantly changing priorities	Focused priorities characterized by dedicated resources and ongoing performance measures
Ignoring people as the key link to strategy implementation	Building core competencies within the organization and its people

businesses large and small have also applied poorly conceived implementation approaches, most often producing limited results. Because the traditional implementation scenario described earlier is all too familiar in most organizations, it is no wonder that strategies are seldom realized. There are alternatives, however, to conventional, ineffective approaches. As companies receive ever more guidance in setting their strategies, management continues to struggle with the question, How do we make our strategy work? The Making Strategy Work model presents a logical framework for facilitating the effective implementation of a company's strategy. The chapters that follow provide case examples, research findings, and a sound project approach—including tools and templates—that offer the guidance in strategy implementation that management is seeking.

Chapter Two

Strategy Implementation

A Pattern Emerges

The twelve organizational influence systems listed in Figure 1.4 were identified after reviewing two main data sources: (1) current research evidence supporting the hypothesis that aligning an organization's influence systems with the business strategy improves organizational performance, and (2) case examples from companies of various sizes and in diverse industries that have taken steps to implement their strategies by realigning the influence systems. From these sources emerged a pattern of three core elements of successful strategy implementation:

1. Management does more than just issue an edict or make a few grand announcements about a company's future direction; it utilizes the organization's influence systems to align its workforce with the strategy, enabling management and employees to support and act on plans.

2. Management aligns more than just one or two of the influence systems; rather, they apply *integrated sets* of the influence systems that in their view are the most important for aligning their workforce with the business strategy and that they believe will have the greatest impact on creating the competencies and behaviors necessary in their organization.

3. Companies that have taken an integrated approach to realigning their influence systems have enjoyed better-than-average performance.

Utilizing the Influence Systems

Utilizing the organization's influence systems to align its workforce with the strategy is the first core element of effective strategy implementation. Some examples follow.

Goals and Measures, Rewards and Recognition

Effective strategy implementation goes much further than communicating a new direction. For example, the performance management process—goals and measures, and rewards and recognition—is crucial to effecting strategic change.

Some people purport that organizations can be changed by simply changing what you measure (see McSparran and Edmunds, 1996; Zamanou and Glasser, 1994). Although this viewpoint oversimplifies the matter, there can be little argument that measurement sends a strong message to employees about what is expected of them, and that clear goals and performance measures can have a significant impact on getting people to act on a strategy. Likewise, performance feedback communicates to employees what management regards as important. For instance, Jack Welch of GE states, "We give our people 360-degree evaluations, with input from superiors, peers, and subordinates. These are the roughest evaluations you can get, because people hear things about themselves they've never heard before. But they get the input they need, and then the chance to improve. If they don't improve, they have to go" (Sherman, 1993, p. 84).

An aspect of performance management that receives a great deal of attention is the role that rewards and recognition play in bringing about strategic change. In fact, the book *1001 Ways to Reward Your Employees*, by Robert Nelson (1994), has become one of the best-selling business books of recent years. Nelson presents anecdotes describing rewards that companies of all sizes and in all industries can use. Although the book is extremely useful in stimulating the reader's thinking about various rewards and means of recognition, its largest drawbacks are that it does not indicate which reward options are the most successful, nor does it discuss how companies can use the alternatives presented in a coordinated way.

Another work on rewards, *The Reward Plan Advantage*, by Jerry McAdams (1996), provides a comprehensive illustration of how to use rewards and recognition successfully to achieve strategic organizational change. Throughout the book, McAdams presents descriptions and examples of implementing reward plans more effectively through the use of education, communications, and assessment; a case for using group-based rewards in addition to or in place of a portion of traditional compensation; an approach to improving the return on reward-plan investment; and a discussion of "best principles" (versus cookie-cutter best practices) relative to rewards and recognition.

There are other clear examples of the use of rewards and recognition to bring about strategic change. For example, the relationship between pay and competency development within organizations has received much attention lately. The traditional path of paying people for particular jobs is quickly being replaced by paying for skills and competencies (Wallace and Crandall, 1996). Also, Watson Wyatt's practice director of executive compensation, Ira Kay (1995), discusses the techniques being used to link executive pay with company performance, and the trend toward providing incentives and stock to lower levels within companies. Kay states, "I think there's going to be continuous pressure to push incentives and stock lower in the organization, e.g., team-based incentives, stock options for virtually all employees, and so forth. My understanding is that when adding incentives, companies do not cut back on the size of existing pay elements. But though the cost of the pay package may rise, I definitely believe that these plans do work and that the improved performance will more than offset the higher cost" (pp. 3–4).

Communications

Communicating is critical to any strategy implementation process. In fact, much of the writing on strategic change has focused on communication as a key element of the process (see, for example, Dobrzynski, 1996; Bott and Hill, 1994; and Sherman, 1993). But implementing strategy is more than issuing a one-time declaration from the president or CEO about a company's goals. Effective communication continually reinforces a company's direction and its progress toward achieving it.

For example, ongoing communications activities were essential to the success of strategy implementation efforts at a division of AT&T Global Business Communications Systems (GBCS). The communications process at GBCS included discussions between senior management and employees through a weekly "ask the president" phone-in forum (Nellis and Lane, 1995). Likewise, according to Stratford Sherman (1993), each of the CEOs involved in a discussion about strategic change in their companies—Jack Welch of General Electric, Lawrence Bossidy of AlliedSignal, William Weiss of Ameritech, and Michael Walsh of Tenneco—attests that continuous communication about the strategic change process is a crucial ingredient of success.

Training and Development

Another crucial component in strategy implementation is training and development. FirstMerit bank, for example, in addition to incentive compensation and revised goals, conducted extensive sales training as part of their strategy implementation effort. The training began with teaching seventy-five managers how to coach tellers. In turn, the managers led approximately five hundred employees through two days of classes on selling financial services (Zack, 1996). Commenting on this training, Carrie Tolstedt, a senior vice president at FirstMerit, states, "Every banker, customer service manager, and teller manager went through that training. . . . When you teach them to listen to what are the customers' needs, and you deliver to that, you get a much more satisfied customer" (Zack, 1996, p. 4A).

Fiat developed a leadership training program that teaches managers to enhance employee efforts and channel them in desired directions, to obtain ideas from staff and ensure that employees participate in continuous improvement, and to accept changes in operations that employ cross-functional work in flat team structures (Auteri, 1994). Ben Pitman (1994) focuses on the use of education to keep management and employee skills apace with rapidly changing technology. He states, "Since we can't slow down technology, our only recourse is to find ways to increase our knowledge base . . . develop an education plan and provide some kind of recognition or celebration when people complete it" (p. 27).

Organizational Structure

Organizational structure changes also appear in many of the case examples of strategic change. Judith Dobrzynski (1996), Jeffrey Zack (1996), Elizabeth Canna (1995), Stratford Sherman (1993), and John Kotter and James Heskett (1992) identify organizational structure changes as part of the strategy implementation efforts at Sears, FirstMerit, Royal Nedlloyd Group, GE, Nissan, and Imperial Chemical Industries (ICI). For example, FirstMerit restructured to improve efficiency in order to capitalize on the "super community banking structure that lowers costs by processing back office tasks centrally" (Zack, 1996). Nissan created a coordinating group called the Product Market Strategy Division at company headquarters to integrate functions involved in designing, producing, testing, and marketing a car (Kotter and Heskett, 1992). And to force decisions to be made closer to the market, chairman Sir John Harvey-Jones reorganized ICI's divisions into nine worldwide businesses, with four headquartered outside the United Kingdom (Kotter and Heskett, 1992).

Senior Leadership

The impact of senior leadership on a successful strategy implementation effort cannot be overlooked. For instance, Sandy Nellis and Fred Lane (1995) provide a detailed description of the strategic change leadership provided by two consecutive presidents of AT&T's GBCS division, Jerre Stead and Patricia Russo. The situation at the beginning of Stead's tenure was one of demoralized employees, a weak financial picture, and pending layoffs. Stead began by presenting the organization with a clear vision of the strategic changes he wanted to see. He wanted to "reexamine every aspect of our people dimension. Engage the workforce. Create an environment that supports our people as our only sustainable, competitive advantage. In other words, make people a key priority" (p. 72). The actions that Stead, and subsequently Russo, *personally* took part in to achieve this vision included, as mentioned earlier, a weekly "ask the president" phone forum, and a new performance management system for all management, including themselves and the other members of the executive team, with revised goals, measures, feedback mechanisms, and rewards.

Sherman (1993) also identifies senior leadership as being a key component of the strategy implementation process. He presents an overview of the strategic change approaches taken by the CEO's of GE (Jack Welch), AlliedSignal (Lawrence Bossidy), Ameritech (William Weiss), and Tenneco (Michael Walsh). Each of these leaders is described by Sherman as being a "corporate revolutionary" (p. 82). About his personal participation in the change efforts at GE, Jack Welch states, "My job is to listen to, search for, think of, and spread ideas, to expose people to good ideas and role models. I'm almost a maitre d', getting the crowd to come sit at this table: 'Enjoy the food here. Try it. See if it tastes good.' And they do. When self-confident people see a good idea, they love it" (p. 84).

Numerous other examples reinforce the importance of senior leadership in successful strategy implementation (see McSparran and Edmunds, 1996; Zack, 1996; Shoesmith, 1996; O'Toole, 1995; Rapaille, 1995; Stewart, 1994; Kotter and Heskett, 1992; and Koestenbaum, 1991). Kotter and Heskett (1992) summarize their introduction on the topic of strategic change by stating, "Without leadership, purposeful change of any magnitude is almost impossible" (p. 99). Finally, at an Internet site called *Frequently Asked Questions About Organizational Change: Answers to Questions Often Asked By Heads of Companies* (Chaudron, 1997, p. 1), a key question is raised: How do I obtain commitment to our plans from my organization? The answer given is through *leadership*.

Rules and Policies

Revising rules and policies also plays a key role in strategy implementation. For example, at Sears, CEO Arthur Martinez scrapped the company's old 29,000 page manual of rules and procedures and replaced it with a brief folder entitled *Freedoms and Obligations*. Measuring about an eighth of an inch thick, the folder contains a one-page letter from Martinez, a one-page list of "shared beliefs"; a sixteen-page booklet outlining leadership principles for managers (such as reward people who add value to Sears), and a seventeen-page code of business conduct for every employee (Dobrzynski, 1996). Other examples of using revised rules and policies as part of strategic change efforts can be found at Ameritech and GE. For instance, Ameritech did away with absurd rules such as not permitting customers to put a plastic cover on a telephone directory once they had it in their own homes. And Jack Welch comments on the bureaucratic organization that grew out of the success experienced by post–World War II GE. He states, "There's a fine line between self-confidence and arrogance. Success often breeds both, along with a reluctance to change. The *bureaucracy* builds up. The people start to believe they're invulnerable. Before they know it, the world changes and they've got to react" (Sherman, 1993, p. 85, emphasis added).

Physical Environment

To facilitate strategic changes, many organizations also transform their *physical environment*. For example, Sears moved out of their tower in downtown Chicago, which allowed groups access to one another only by riding the elevator to other floors. The company has moved to a new headquarters building in suburban Chicago with only a few levels and many open spaces, allowing much easier movement between groups than the multistoried tower (Dobrzynski, 1996). Other organizations use "virtual offices" to encourage people to work outside of their facilities and closer to their customers (Caldwell and Gambon, 1996). In addition, numerous organizations use wall hangings such as posters and electronic message boards to communicate key strategic credos and information to employees on an ongoing basis.

Staffing, Selection, and Succession

One of the most overused clichés in business, but also one of the most important aspects of supporting a growth strategy, is to have the right people in the right place at the right time doing the right things. At no time is staffing, selection, and succession as important to a company as during growth. In fact, the percentage of CEOs who identified a shortage of skilled, trained workers as their top barrier to achieving desired growth rose from approximately 38 percent in 1993 to more than 60 percent in 1996 ("More Help Wanted," 1996). Companies are now expanding their use of technology in hiring, implementing new approaches to selection, and applying succession planning to maintain a ready pool of talented management.

Gillian Flynn (1996), for example, describes the application of technology at Cisco Systems, a rapidly growing $1.9 billion (1995 revenues) technology company based in San Jose, California. During 1996, Cisco added 1,200 to 1,500 jobs per quarter. To help facilitate the process, Cisco implemented a human resources home page on the Internet to recruit candidates on-line. The page includes information on compensation and benefits, internship and mentoring programs, community contributions programs, and job listings.

To pursue service strategies, companies are looking to hire people who possess customer-friendly attributes. Gaston (1996) recommends that a selection process for service employees focus on *critical indicators of competency* (such as friendliness and an outgoing and energetic attitude). Although he does not recommend a particular instrument, Gaston also advocates that the indicators should be validated with a formal testing instrument as part of the screening process. Another increasingly used method of applicant screening is to put people through a job "audition." To assess potential fit, some companies are now requiring that candidates be hired for temporary tryout periods before being offered a permanent position (Dahle, 1996). In addition, many companies are directing more attention to building management competency by establishing a pool of talent from which they can draw, and in order to pursue strategies that call for growth in regions beyond U.S. borders, companies are including greater numbers of management with international backgrounds and experiences. Dutton (1996) cites examples of formal succession planning processes at Corning, DynCorp, Wal-Mart, Tenneco, and Coca-Cola, among others. Although many companies are doing a good job of instituting succession processes, only 42 percent of companies surveyed in 1995 by the American Management Association said they have a succession plan in place for their CEO, 37 percent said they have such a plan for senior management, 28 percent have a plan for selected middle management and supervisors, and only 18 percent have a plan for selected technical and professional positions (Peak, 1996, p. 24).

Information Systems and Knowledge Sharing

As part of their growth strategies, many organizations are revising their information systems and knowledge sharing processes. Organizations large and small are installing information systems that facilitate knowledge transfer among employees and management. Companies such as Dow Chemical, Scandinavian financial services company Skandia Group, and Harris Corporation have installed knowledge management systems and processes (Mullin, 1996). For example, Dow began by undertaking the job of systematically managing its portfolio of approximately 30,000 patents. Then management realized that the process went well beyond patent control into management of various kinds of knowledge throughout many departments and manufacturing facilities. Likewise, Skandia Group views knowledge management as an organic process and believes that the real task is to develop a system that forms the knowledge base of the company. The first step is building an internal database, or "intranet." Companies take several approaches to database development, including customized systems built in-house or by consultants, and off-the-shelf packages. Many smaller companies that cannot afford to build and maintain their own intranet can outsource their knowledge database to an outside provider. No matter what approach is taken, there are extensive implications for management and employees alike in order to make the process of knowledge sharing work. Simply installing an organization-wide database and expecting people to openly welcome and, more important, use it effectively is a fantasy.

Operational and Process Changes

Operational and process changes have been in the forefront of company strategies for the past several years. Recently, operational changes have yielded substantial increases in performance for companies across various industries. For example, Joseph Weber (1996) describes the operational transition known as *Demand Flow Technology* (D.F.T.) at American Standard. He describes the approach as a means of dramatically improving production efficiency. It has enabled American Standard to reduce costs, cut manufacturing cycles in half, and decrease inventories by almost 30 percent. Moreover, the company is now beginning to apply D.F.T. to office-based work. They have dismantled private offices to put people together who need to share ideas and make decisions more quickly. Likewise, *flexible production* has been determined to be the core competency that provided the competitive advantage for Japanese auto manufacturers throughout the 1970s and 1980s (Womack, Jones, and Roos, 1990). Similarly, in the garment industry, *modular production* (forming small teams of people who work together to assemble garments) reduces apparel production time to as little as a few hours, compared to several days for traditional production systems (Gephart, 1995).

Ceremonies and Events

Finally, organizations often deliberately conduct ceremonies and events to reinforce strategic changes. For example, Sears holds sessions for managers and employees called the "PSE [Pure Selling Environment] Circus." These events, complete with a ringmaster and clowns, are akin to pep rallies designed to disseminate to employees information about what the company is doing in such areas as customer service (Dobrzynski, 1996). At Nissan, management wanted to bring the company closer to the customer in very direct ways. One effort they implemented was "Open Days," when people outside the company are allowed to come into the plants and walk around. Tandem Computers' management regularly celebrates achievements at Friday afternoon events. And the Milwaukee-based Northwestern Mutual life insurance company holds a three-day event every summer for all agents and headquarters employees. The main component of this event is a Broadway-like show starring the CEO and other company executives that includes a skit designed to overtly emphasize the organization's core values, and that contains a lot of recognition of individual employees who exemplify those values (Kotter and Heskett, 1992).

Applying Integrated Sets of Influence Systems

The second core element in the pattern of effective strategy implementation is that management applies *integrated sets* of the twelve influence systems that in its view are the most important for aligning the company's workforce with its business strategy. No one distinctive subset of the twelve influence systems appears at this point to provide the best route of strategy implementation. What is important is that management apply more than just a new pay program or some different training to make the strategy work.

Several single-industry and cross-industry studies have identified that integrated sets of human resources practices create multiple reinforcements for motivation and skill development (see MacDuffie, 1995; Berg and others, 1995; Arthur, 1994; Huselid, 1995; and Ichniowski, 1995). Moreover, each of these studies found that interconnected work and human resources practices lead to improved company financial performance, and that new work organization coupled with human resources management practices can have major positive effects on productivity and quality. Collectively the findings also suggest that peripheral changes to singular practices have marginal or no impact on company performance. Furthermore, no single collection of practices leading to higher company performance has been identified to date.

In addition to the research data, several case examples exist to support the application of integrated groupings of the twelve influence systems. For instance, one widely publicized strategic shift is the transformation taking place at Sears under the direction of CEO Arthur Martinez. He has refocused Sears on the core retail business and has been improving the look and service of the stores as key growth strategies. To implement the strategy, Sears has realigned at least eight of the twelve influence systems. For example, it has redesigned its *performance management* approach. Managers now receive 360-degree feedback, and bonuses for the top two hundred executives are no longer based solely on financial measures. Revenues, return on assets, and operating margins are the basis for only half of executive incentives. The other half is equally dependent upon customer satisfaction measures and employee ratings of management. Additionally, the *physical environment* has been changed by converting the store offices of individual department supervisor into a shared team space, which encourages supervisors to spend more time out on the selling floor providing feedback and coaching to sales associates about sales behaviors and techniques. Sears has also employed the *communications* and *ceremonies and events* influence systems by conducting the PSE Circus described earlier. Their *rules and policies* have been revamped by replacing the old Sears policy manual with the *Freedoms and Obligations* booklet also described earlier. *Training* on customer service has been provided to management, supervisors, and employees across the company, and new *job descriptions and operating structures* have been implemented to place decision making closer to the customer (Dobrzynski, 1996).

Another example of realigning integrated sets of the influence systems comes from the Royal Nedlloyd Group, a $3.5 billion shipping company based in Rotterdam, the Netherlands. To accomplish the company's turnaround strategy, Nedlloyd's management redesigned no fewer than seven of the influence systems. Management realigned the *organization's structure* and *rules and policies*, making the corporate logistics unit the coordinator of the company's operating units. It also realigned *goals and measures* and *rewards and recognition* to focus on accountability and profitability. The *information systems and knowledge sharing* and the *operational/process changes* influence systems were put in place in the form of a database that allows the entire company to identify which of Nedlloyd's units is doing business with certain clients, and to identify gaps on which the company can capitalize. Meetings are held every month among the account managers of the various operating units to share customer information. Additionally, *communications* and *training* were employed that focused on the new operating procedures being put in place.

Similarly, management at Southwest Airlines has employed most of the influence systems to implement a strategy of quality, flexibility, and superior customer service. The workplace has few rigid *rules*, and the company *rewards* employees through a profit sharing plan and emphasizes customer service in *performance appraisals* and *communications*. Additionally, extensive *training* is provided to the entire workforce. The mechanics, customer service, operations, reservations, and other divisions all provide their own

technical training, and all employees participate in courses on customer service, decision making, safety, and career development
(Gephart, 1995).

The Results Speak for Themselves

Many people ask, Where does all this lead? What is the bottom-line
payoff? The answer is found in the third core element of successful
strategy implementation—*organizational performance*. The performance achieved by the companies identified in this chapter bears
out the hypothesis that aligning an organization's influence systems
in order to create necessary behaviors and competencies promotes
a company's ability to implement it's strategy and achieve desired
business results. For example, since 1992, Sears has seen its market
share, operating margins, and inventory turnover all rise, while
overhead as a percentage of sales has fallen (Dobrzynski, 1996).
Likewise, the Royal Nedlloyd Group reported a net profit of $61
million in 1994, compared to a loss of $74 million in 1993, and it
paid a cash dividend ($.83 per share) for the first time since 1989.
Since then, the company has remained in the black and it is well
positioned for its 1997 merger with P&O Lines of Great Britain
(Canna, 1995). AT&T's GBCS identifies associate value (the development opportunities managers provide for their employees)
and profitable growth as key measures of success. From 1991 to
1994, the division saw a 62 percent improvement in associate value
ratings, and shareholder value gains in the form of market-share
growth, revenue increases, and a decrease in overall operating expenses (Nellis and Lane, 1995). And while most airlines have struggled to turn a profit in recent years, Southwest has excelled. Its
excellence is measured not only by operating profit (it was the only
airline to show a profit in 1992, and the leading airline in net income over the three years following) but by other measures as well.
Southwest flew more passengers per employee and had the fewest
employees per aircraft in 1991, and it had the second lowest cost per
available seat mile in 1993. Moreover, the company's employee

turnover rate is only 7 percent (the lowest in the industry), and for three years running (1993–1995) the U.S. Department of Transportation determined that Southwest had the most on-time flights, the best baggage-handling rating, and the highest customer satisfaction ratings. A six-person ground crew is used to ready a plane in fifteen minutes, compared to an average of one hour for other airlines (Gephart, 1995).

Recent research focusing on using influence systems to achieve workforce and strategy alignment also provides evidence of increased organizational performance. For instance, John MacDuffie (1995) identified three sets of interrelated practices in the auto industry that create mutually reinforcing support for employee motivation and skill, thus producing high performance: (1) manufacturing practices, (2) work-systems practices, and (3) human resources practices. MacDuffie found that auto assembly plants that use flexible production systems along with high-commitment human resources practices outperformed traditional mass-production systems in both productivity and quality. In a study of the apparel industry, Peter Berg and others (1995) examined the performance differences between *bundle production systems* and *modular production*. The bundle system breaks down assembly into separate tasks, each focusing on one piece of a garment and completed by one person. The material is moved from assembly person to assembly person in bundles of pieces—hence the name. The bundle system is prone to quality problems, low flexibility for style changes, and slow production. Modular production, by contrast, uses a small team of people to assemble each garment. It takes the team only a few hours to produce the same number of items of clothing that it takes workers in the bundle system several days to assemble. The modular system requires that people be cross-trained and that they contribute to improving the quality of the garments. It involves practices such as multiskilling, job rotation, group incentives, skill-based pay, extensive training, and fewer supervisors. Berg's findings indicate that modular production in apparel manufacturing results in greater quality and productivity than the bundle system.

In a study of the steel industry, Jeffrey Arthur (1994) examined the impact of high-commitment human resources systems on performance and employee turnover at minimills. Arthur identified systems that place emphasis on employee development and commitment to the company as being *commitment systems*. He characterized *control human resources systems* as those that focus on cost reduction and efficiency. Arthur's findings suggest that achieving a strategy of differentiation, that is, being differentiated from competitors on the basis of superior quality or outstanding service, for example, requires a corresponding commitment to maximizing human resources strategy. Likewise, accomplishing a low-cost strategy necessitates a corresponding cost-reduction human resources strategy at the minimills. Arthur also found that steel companies with human resources systems that emphasize commitment to the firm experienced lower turnover rates, less scrap, and higher productivity than companies with human resources systems that emphasize efficiency and reduced labor costs.

Evidence of the positive impacts of aligning a company's influence systems with its business strategy also exists in cross-industry studies. For instance, Mark Huselid (1995) surveyed 3,400 firms with more than one hundred employees across various industries. He identified two sets of practices associated with high-performance work environments: employee motivation and employee skills. He found that companies who invest in high-performance work practices enjoy lower employee turnover, higher productivity, and better overall financial performance. In another cross-industry study, Casey Ichniowski (1990) analyzed the impact of personnel practices on productivity and stock market performance in 200 U.S. manufacturing companies. He categorized companies according to six primary human resources practices: (1) flexible versus narrow job design, (2) merit-based versus seniority-based promotions, (3) percentage of non-entry-level jobs filled from within, (4) formal training programs, (5) formal grievance procedures, and (6) other communications and information mechanisms. The types of companies categorized by Ichniowski were traditional union systems, small-business systems with no formal practices or policies, and high-commitment systems distinguished by flexible job design, formal training and communications programs, and high levels of internal promotions. His findings led to three main conclusions: (1) companies with the best performance have high-commitment systems; (2) companies with flexible job design but no formal training programs have significantly lower productivity and poorer stock performance; and (3) organizations must adopt all of the practices of a high-commitment system if they are to experience performance advantages, and training is a critical component.

Conclusion

The core hypothesis of this chapter, and indeed of this book, is that there is a critical relationship between aligning an organization's influence systems to create necessary behaviors and competencies and a company's ability to implement its strategy and achieve desired business results. The recent research and literature on workforce alignment with business strategy are by no means comprehensive; for example, a search for work published since 1990 on strategy implementation identified fewer than thirty relevant entries, most of which were case examples of organizations' general change or culture change efforts. Nevertheless, the research and literature that do exist show that companies do employ variations of the twelve influence systems to accomplish strategic change, which bears out the hypothesis and provides a good foundation for identifying the positive performance results that can be achieved (see Appendix D for a tabular synopsis of the current research on this topic). More systematic examination needs to be done, however.

A secondary hypothesis—that a particular subset of the twelve influence systems has the greatest impact on effectively implementing an organization's strategy and producing subsequent business results—is also crucial and requires further study. If this hypothesis were found to be true, it would help management to focus its time, effort, and dollars on a set of influence systems that would provide the greatest return on investment. Additionally, by focusing efforts on a subgroup of the twelve influence systems, the time frames for strategy implementation would be shortened—an effect that management in today's fast-changing world would fully appreciate.

Throughout the next part of *Making Strategy Work*, a pragmatic step-by-step process for strategy implementation is presented. Chapters Three through Nine detail the steps an organization can take to accomplish a coordinated effort that clarifies the key components and goals of the business strategy; identifies the workforce behaviors and competencies needed to achieve the strategy; determines which of the twelve influence systems will provide the greatest impact in building those behaviors and competencies; redesigns the selected influence systems to create the greatest workforce alignment and produce the maximum business results; and implements, measures, and refines the strategy implementation process.

Part Two

Realignment and Implementation

A Project Approach

Chapter Three

Getting Organized and Establishing the Project

Although it's worth the effort, strategy implementation is a complex process in companies large and small. This complexity stems from three main factors. First, the twelve influence systems are systemic and interactive, and as already noted, changing one of them impacts at least one of the others. For instance, redesigning goals and measures creates implications for, at the very least, communications, training, rewards and recognition, and rules and policies. Second, most if not all of the influence systems already exist in organizations, and redesigning these systems captures everyone's attention and is often seen both positively and negatively at any given time, depending on who you ask. Third, the method of realigning the influence systems for a particular part of an organization may not be what is best for other parts of the organization. For example, realigning the influence systems to focus a sales force on better selling skills and techniques should be different from realigning the systems in a manufacturing function, where productivity and quality are desired. Because of these inherent complexities, it is better to address strategy implementation by design rather than by chance. Applying the same discipline throughout deployment as is applied to the formation of plans makes successful implementation much more likely. A pragmatic *project approach* to strategy implementation is necessary.

Project Flow: Six Stages

Whether the organization is large (more than ten thousand employees), small (under one thousand employees), or in between, strategy implementation should be addressed through organized project stages. Figure 3.1 illustrates the six project stages of the Making Strategy Work process. These stages are *one approach* to strategy implementation. There are others. However, following the Making Strategy Work process brings rigor and integration to an effort that is often ad hoc, uncoordinated, and segmented—which is why most strategy implementation efforts fail. The six-stage process is logical, and it has been tested in organizations of various sizes and in various geographies and industries. It quickly engages a broad base of senior and middle management and employees. It is not designed to put a small group of select people behind closed doors for several months until they emerge into the daylight with the "right" answer.

As Figure 3.1 illustrates, the process begins with establishing the project. Next, the initial project participants clarify the business strategy, identify the competencies and behaviors that management and employees will need to achieve the strategy, and determine which influence systems will need to be realigned to create the necessary competencies and behaviors and drive toward the business

Figure 3.1 The Six Stages of the Making Strategy Work Project

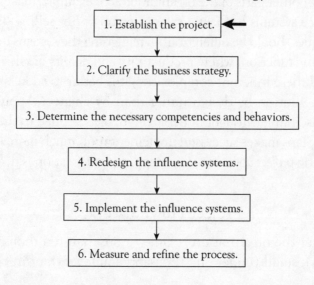

strategy. The project then engages a broader group of people in task forces assigned to redesign the selected influence systems. These *realignment task forces* are charged with developing changes to the influence systems, detailing implementation plans for the redesigned systems, and identifying the measures that will be used to track implementation success. The final stage of the process requires the task forces to assist with implementing the redesigned influence systems, measuring their effectiveness, and refining them based on the effectiveness measures. Throughout the process, a *project manager* and *project core team* are responsible for keeping the process moving and organized, and for ensuring that the influence system redesigns developed by the task forces are coordinated and organized.

This chapter presents the first stage in the process—establishing the project.

Project Management

Sound project management is crucial to addressing the complexities of strategy implementation in organizations consisting of varying functions, divisions, and locations. It becomes the critical nerve center for coordinating a process comprising several manageable subprojects that will result in strategy implementation. Some companies have stumbled into strategy implementation without even knowing it. But whether their approach has been intentional or otherwise, companies that have successfully implemented strategies can trace their success back to specific, tangible subprojects. For example, in a large high-tech firm, management moved the company to be more quality and customer oriented and more responsive. Over a three-year span it became obvious that the strategy had been implemented as a result of successfully completing a series of focused subprojects, including

- The implementation of a new quality system that included procedures for tracking and responding to customer complaints

- The redesign of the performance review and bonus system to include support for the new quality system
- A reduction of manufacturing cycle time through the identification and elimination of steps that had little or no value
- A move to a newer, larger facility
- The development of new selection and hiring procedures that focused on bringing in more educated, professional support staff

Each of these changes was conducted as a project under the responsibility of a particular functional area or a cross-functional team. The compelling factor is that strategy implementation was not the primary goal of these projects. They were originally undertaken by various managers as "fixes" that were needed within the company. Moreover, none of the projects alone actually created the successful strategy implementation. But collectively, their net effect was positive changes in operational productivity and financial performance, which were key goals of the company's strategy. The real question is whether management could have deployed the strategy faster and more effectively by viewing the projects as an integrated, coordinated strategy implementation effort.

Good project management for strategy implementation is similar to managing any effective project, large or small. Three key project management elements that must be addressed are (1) the project *structure* (What infrastructure will support and facilitate the successful progress and completion of the project?), (2) the project *tasks* (How can the large effort be broken down into logical tasks or subprojects?), and (3) the project *tracking and measurement* (What project measures will indicate progress and allow us to adjust the project as we go? How should the project measures and progress be tracked?). Failure to address these three elements and apply solid project management disciplines to them will only create confusion and a haphazard, unproductive undertaking.

Project Structure

A project structure must be developed to address critical questions such as Who is going to work on the implementation effort? Who will be the project manager? What project reporting relationships should exist? Where and how will decisions be made? and In what ways and how frequently will project participants communicate with one another?

Figure 3.2 illustrates the structure of a typical Making Strategy Work project. Participants include an advisory team, a sponsor, a project manager, a core team, and several alignment task forces (ATFs). The roles fulfilled by each of the project participants are summarized in Figure 3.3. As noted earlier, making strategy work is not a side issue for management, nor should the project be a parallel activity for people while they are "running the business."

Figure 3.2 Structure of a Typical Making Strategy Work Project

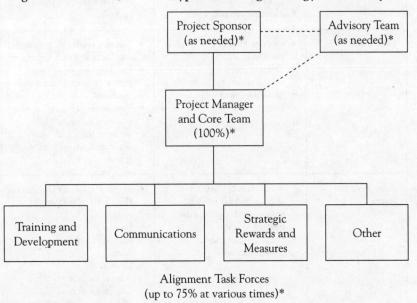

*Typical time commitment of participant(s)

Figure 3.3 Roles and Responsibilities
of Making Strategy Work Project Participants

Project Constituent	Roles	Sample Tasks
Advisory team	• Are vocal, visible leaders of the strategy deployment effort • Provide oversight, direction, and review • Participate in the delivery of key messages	• Present strategy implementation messages in key meetings throughout company • Assist the project sponsor in selecting the project manager and core team members • Meet with the core team for regular progress reviews
Project sponsor	• Has day-to-day oversight of project progress • Assists core team with key decisions (for example, task force overlaps that cannot be resolved by the core team)	• Present key messages in meetings with the advisory team • Communicate with managers to free up resources to staff the project
Project manager	• Oversees project planning and coordination • Communicates project progress • Manages the core team	• Develop project Gantt chart • Conduct core team meetings • Provide regular progress updates to the project sponsor
Core team	• Oversee project coordination • Oversee project communication • Lead alignment task forces	• Oversee selection, staffing, and kickoff of task forces • Hold regular meetings to review progress reports and measures • Present progress and recommendations to the advisory team and other organizational entities as scheduled
Alignment task forces	• Work on subprojects to align particular influence systems with the business strategy • Participate in project communication	• Prepare a plan for changes to their particular influence system • Present recommendations to the core team and advisory team • Coordinate and communicate with other task forces as needed to address overlaps and gaps

Making strategy work *is* running the business. Consequently, the project structure often fits the existing management structure of the organization. For example, in a large electronics catalogue retailer, the project sponsor was the chief operating officer (COO), the project manager was a senior manager from one of the operating units, and the advisory team members were the operating and functional executives of the company (that is, the business unit heads and the senior vice presidents from human resources, legal, finance, and so forth).

The Advisory Team

The project advisory team is typically composed of several if not all of the most senior executives in the company, often including the chief executive officer (CEO) or president, the COO, other senior vice presidents in charge of operating units, and vice presidents of functions such as human resources, finance, systems, and so on. For effectiveness, the team should be no larger than six to eight members.

The roles of the advisory team include providing guidance and direction to the core team, making key decisions regarding recommendations coming out of the core team and ATFs, and delivering communications to the organization about the progress and expectations of the strategy implementation effort. For the advisory team to fulfill its roles successfully, the typical time commitment of the participants throughout the deployment process is "as needed." However, each member of the team should be prepared to participate in update and review sessions (two to four formal review sessions and several informal sessions) with the core team, and to participate in the delivery of face-to-face communications with the organization. Appendix A presents an advisory team guidebook that can be used to orient the advisory team and that can serve as a reference tool for them throughout the Making Strategy Work process.

The Project Sponsor

The role of the project sponsor is crucial for the progression and accomplishment of the project. The sponsor should be a senior executive who is well respected within the organization and who has a broad, strategic view of the company. The sponsor also participates as a member of the advisory team. He or she can be either the CEO, the COO, or a senior vice president, but should not be below this level in the organization. Like the advisory team's commitment, the sponsor's time commitment to the project is as needed. However, the sponsor should participate in the update and review sessions with the core and advisory teams, and be available to the project-manager and core teams.

A key role of the sponsor is to assist the project manager and core team by creating access to the various organizational areas. Also, the sponsor can assist the core team with day-to-day project decisions that are not significant enough to bring to the entire advisory team. As the project hits roadblocks, as it inevitably will, the sponsor can help the core team or task forces to deal with the issue. To fulfill his or her role successfully, the project sponsor should be readily available to the project manager and other project team members.

The Project Manager

Project managers often must operate at two levels: day-to-day activity tracking and progress monitoring, and overall project coordination. Performing these two roles implies two types of project manager profiles. Day-to-day project tracking requires excellent planning and organizing abilities. To fulfill this role, a project manager needs to put in place project planning and tracking tools and project reporting and communications mechanisms, including *Gannt chart time lines* (to show what tasks and activities happen when), *key project milestones* (to identify the major periodic project events and/or deliverables), *accountability assignments* (to indicate who does what), *meeting agendas* (to identify meeting objectives, attendees, time frames, locations, and topics), *communication and reporting procedures* (to describe who gets updated about project progress, and how and when), and *project budgets and resources allocations* (to establish how many people and facilities and how much equipment and so on are needed, and the associated costs).

In project coordination the project manager marshals resources where and when needed, diffuses disputes that can arise along the way, and acts as the "orchestra conductor" for all of the project entities. This level of project management activity is more dynamic than the project tracking activities just described and is often more akin to art than science. The marshaling of resources involves identifying the knowledge, skills, and abilities needed for various project tasks, estimating how much time will need to be dedicated to each task, and determining where the appropriate people can be obtained either within or outside of the organization. The project manager often must help free up appropriate resources from their current work; continuous reallocation of resources is often necessary to make sure that the areas of the project needing more help receive it and that the areas that can spare resources do so. Dispute resolution may be needed at various times, because the ideas and recommendations of various project participants will not always be harmonious. The project manager can act as intermediary in these cases, helping to resolve the disagreements that inevitably occur along the way. Project orchestration—determining the sequencing of events, deciding when to accelerate or decelerate parts of the project, and making sure that the various project entities (the sponsor, the advisory team, the core team, and the task forces) are staying informed, coordinating with one another, and communicating with one another regularly—is often the greatest challenge to the project manager and can take a huge effort.

Excellent project management is a full-time responsibility that is critical to the success of integrated strategy implementation. Many times companies will select two project managers because of the dual role that needs to be filled. For example, a large Canadian

insurance company chose a more senior person to do the project orchestration and a less senior person to perform the day-to-day project tracking and progress monitoring. This added the need to
coordinate another level of communication, but in the long run the
complexity of the project proved that there was enough to contend
with in each role to justify the use of both people.

The Core Team

The project core team is the backbone of the strategy implementation effort. This team should be made up of highly capable people
with varied backgrounds and experiences, including knowledge of
the line businesses and the company's support functions, such as
communications, compensation, training, and the like. To be effective, however, the core team should not consist of more than ten
to twelve people. Including people from various functions and line
organizations on the team is invaluable to the success of the project. Even though many of the influence systems may be overseen
and/or delivered by the human resources function, not having the
deployment be solely a human resources effort is critical to success.
Strategy implementation must be "owned" by the line organizations
as well because line management must take action at various points
to move the process forward. For example, new management techniques such as performance coaching, new methods for staffing and
selection, or redesigned incentive systems all require managers in
line businesses to change how they perform their jobs.

The role of the core team includes performing day-to-day project work (such as conducting analyses, designing new processes, and
so on), coordinating the products produced by the ATFs, carrying
out project communications with the advisory team and other parts
of the organization, leading various ATFs, and implementing the
redesigned influence systems (including logistics, communications,
and required education). To fulfill their roles successfully, the core
team participants typically must commit themselves full-time for

the duration of the project. This time commitment may fluctuate due to the particular needs of the project at any point along the way. Appendix B presents a core team guidebook that can be used to orient the core team and as a reference tool throughout the Making Strategy Work process.

The Alignment Task Forces

Several task forces are established after the core team identifies the influence systems that need to be realigned. For the sake of continuity and communication with the core team, each ATF is led by a member of the core team. Like the core team, the ATFs should be populated by people with content knowledge of the influence systems (such as communications, training, rewards, and so on), as well as people who have knowledge of the line operations and the aims of the business strategy. For efficiency, the ATFs should be kept small (no more than four to seven members). This does not mean, however, that the members of the small groups will be the only ones to work on the redesign of the influence systems. The members of various ATFs will often draw on resources within the organization to assist with the redesign and implementation work.

The role of the ATFs is to do the actual redesign of each priority influence system. Additionally, the ATFs will assist with implementing the redesigned influence systems, including administering the necessary logistics, communication, and education. For the ATFs to be successful, the typical time commitment of the participants should be up to 75 percent (or sometimes more) throughout implementation. This time commitment may fluctuate due to the particular needs of the project at any point along the way. Appendix C presents an alignment task forces guidebook that can be used to orient the ATFs, and that can serve as a reference tool for them throughout the implementation process. Appendix C also includes an implementation planning template that can be used to create consistency among the various ATFs' plans.

The project structure in smaller organizations can involve fewer people than in larger organizations. Beware, however, of the danger that the implementation effort might be seen by the organization as an insular, behind-closed-doors activity. Also, subteams for implementing geographical strategy (such as European, North American, Asian/Pacific, and/or country-specific teams) can be established as part of the project structure to address geographical anomalies. For example, a large multinational manufacturing company based in the United Kingdom used country implementation teams either to adopt the influence system redesigns developed by the core project team and ATFs, or to adjust the redesigns to their local needs based on their country's particular operational strategy.

Project Tasks

Just as a map is important when driving down a new highway, a clear project "road map" is invaluable for guiding the project manager, core team, and other project members through the implementation process. Figure 3.4 illustrates a typical Making Strategy Work project road map, including time frames, formal core team meetings, scheduled core team update sessions with the project sponsor and advisory team, and major work steps for the core team and ATFs.

It should be emphasized that Figure 3.4 represents a *typical* Making Strategy Work path and will be used throughout the next several chapters to illustrate the progress of a representative Making Strategy Work effort. However, as experience has proven time and again, a "typical" project often has unforeseen events that affect progress either positively or negatively. One example of a common variable is project resources, such as the accessibility of key executives for needed input and the availability of core team and task force members to work on the project. Other variables that can influence the progress of a project include the complexity of an organization's current influence systems, the company's geographical diversity, and the skill level of the project manager. Good

Figure 3.4 Typical Making Strategy Work Project Road Map

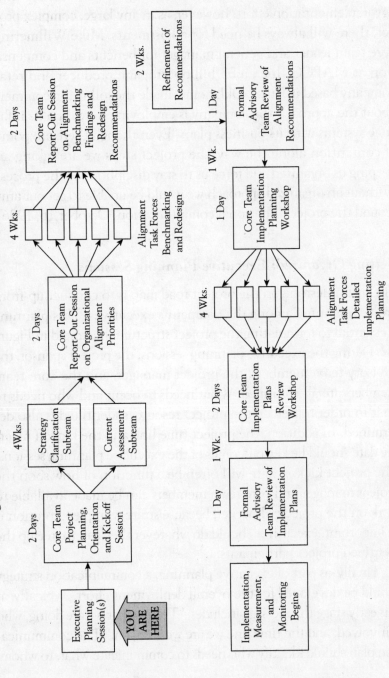

Approximately sixteen weeks from two-day kickoff session to beginning of implementation.

planning goes a long way toward smoothing the wrinkles of a strategy implementation effort; however, as in any large, complex project, there will always be need for adjustments. Mike Willmering, core team leader and general manager for benefits and compensation at MAPCO, Inc., a $3 billion propane producer and retail company based in Tulsa, Oklahoma, made the following comment about the approach the company is employing to realign its influence systems with its business plan: "Even though there are points of contention along the way, the project steps we are taking are keeping us organized and force us to stay disciplined to the process. Without an organized approach we would be unable to get our arms around the project" (personal communication, October 16, 1996).

Getting Organized: Executive Planning Sessions

The first milestone on the project road map is to conduct up-front project planning among the company's executives. This planning is essential to formulating the project structure illustrated in Figure 3.2. During the executive planning sessions, the project sponsor, the advisory team members, the project manager, and the core team members are all identified. What needs to occur and who needs to do it in order to free up the project resources identified is also determined. In addition, the project time line and the kickoff meeting date should be key outcomes of the executive planning sessions. The project kickoff date will often be a function of how soon the project manager and core team members can be made available to work on the project. However, because strategy implementation is so important, executives should do whatever they can to free up the identified project participants.

Finally, as part of executive planning, a communication strategy should be developed for the overall deployment effort. Typically, at this early stage the message includes, "This is what we are doing, who is involved, and the time line we are working on." The communication plan should identify who needs to communicate what, to whom, how, and when. The identified project manager should play a key role in developing the communications strategy, because he or she should ultimately be responsible for ensuring that communications occur as scheduled. Figure 3.5 presents an example of a communications strategy matrix that can be used as a communications planning template throughout the strategy implementation effort.

Getting Started: Core Team Kickoff Session

Figure 3.6 shows that after the executive planning sessions, the next milestone on the project road map is to bring the core team together to kick off the project. This two-day session entails communicating to the core team members the project time line and key milestones, the names of the project participants, project roles and responsibilities, and the project management mechanisms to be used (such as weekly progress reporting, weekly project meetings, cross-team communications, and so on). In addition, during this session the project core team is divided into two project subteams of about six members each that will exist for approximately four weeks. One of the two subteams (known as the *strategy clarification subteam*) is charged with two tasks: clarifying the strategy and identifying the necessary individual and organizational competencies and behaviors. The other subteam (known as the *current assessment subteam*) is given the task of assessing the state of the organizational influence systems as they are currently being applied within the company. The subteam leaders are identified, and cross-team communication is also planned. A sample outline of meeting topics for a core team kickoff session is included in Appendix B.

Interim Project Activities

In addition to the key milestones identified on the project road map, several other activities need to occur throughout the project, including the following:

Figure 3.5 Sample Making Strategy Work Communications Planning Matrix

Stakeholders (Who?)	Objective (Why?)	Message (What?)	Vehicle (How?)	How Often (When?)	Responsibility (Who Delivers?)
Executive Management	Explanation of overall strategy implementation effort	Reasons for a dedicated strategy implementation effort Project structure, goals, objectives, and time line	Meeting	10/01	CEO
All Management and Employees	Explanation of overall strategy implementation effort	Project structure, goals, objectives, and time line	Newsletter E-mail Department meetings	U.S. 10/03 Europe 10/4	Executives

Source: Adapted from Galpin, 1996.

Figure 3.6 Typical Making Strategy Work Road Map: Core Team Kickoff Session

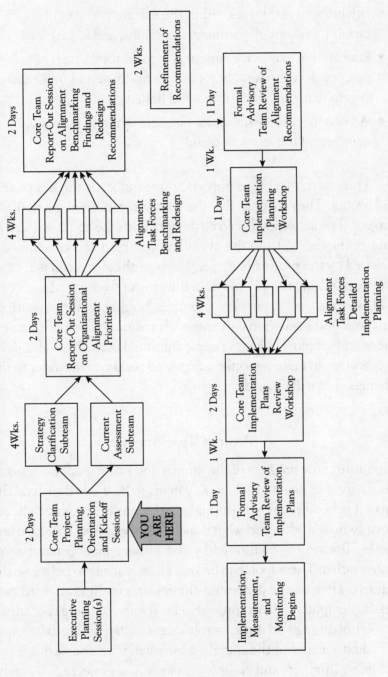

Approximately sixteen weeks from two-day kickoff session to beginning of implementation.

- Communication events with business unit management teams
- Briefings for employees within the various parts of the organization (divisions, departments, locations, and so on)
- Educational events for various groups on topics such as competency development, best-practice findings, and influence system realignment concepts and design
- Ad hoc meetings with senior management and individual members of the advisory team

These activities are as important to conduct as the key project milestones. They are crucial to the communications element of the project. The activities should be put into both the communications matrix (Figure 3.5) and the overall project plan and time line developed by the project manager. Many of these interim activities will demand additional time from the project team members, but it will be time well spent. For example, holding communications briefings and educational events with various groups of management and employees keeps people informed of progress along the way and, even more important, begins to build commitment to the changes that will be made.

Project Tracking

Monitoring the progress of the project and making adjustments as necessary is critical to success. Key items to be tracked include the project schedule, the project budget, the project resource allocations (who is working on what), and adjustments, both needed and made. Tracking is facilitated by the project management tools noted earlier. These tools can be kept electronically to help ease the burden. They can be generated either using traditional word processing, graphics, and/or spreadsheet software, or using specialized project planning and tracking software that can both produce and coordinate many of these tools. Moreover, with the existence of company intranets and groupware, electronic project tools can be more easily shared by project participants, and with other organizational entities as needed.

Conclusion

Key success factors on the front end that will make a strategy implementation effort successful down the road include: selecting a competent and well-respected project manager, allocating sufficient project resources, identifying advisory team members, producing a project schedule, developing a communications plan, and completing other project start-up elements. Unfortunately, efficiently and effectively getting a strategy implementation effort up and running is a process that most organizations do poorly. The consequences of not doing a good job of getting the effort off the ground go beyond a short-term waste of company resources. A badly planned and poorly started effort will have long-lasting negative effects, including limited (if any) success at implementing the business strategy, no true commitment on the part of management or employees to making the strategy work, no realization of business results, and nothing remotely related to building a long-term business growth capability. The message: do what it takes to get the effort started the right way!

Chapter Four

Clarifying the Business Strategy

The second stage in the Making Strategy Work project is clarifying the business strategy (see Figure 4.1). The half of the project core team known as the *strategy clarification subteam*, whose members are identified during the project kickoff meeting, conducts this work.

The Strategy Clarification Team

The members of the strategy clarification subteam need to understand the contents of the business strategy (such as new-market penetration, operating changes, new products, a focus on sales and

**Figure 4.1 The Six Stages of the
Making Strategy Work Project: Stage Two**

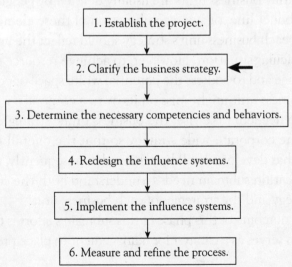

1. Establish the project.

2. Clarify the business strategy.

3. Determine the necessary competencies and behaviors.

4. Redesign the influence systems.

5. Implement the influence systems.

6. Measure and refine the process.

service, enhanced technology, and so on), and its aims (such as revenue growth, increased market share, enhanced profitability, and so on). Figure 4.2 identifies the milestone on the project road map where this effort occurs. The subteam can typically accomplish this work in approximately four weeks, depending on scheduling conflicts, company size, and other variables.

To aid the subteam in their clarification effort, people who were involved in the strategy formulation process should be involved in clarifying the strategy. These people become an internal knowledge source for the subteam, because they have detailed understanding of the contents of the business strategy. A good example of this involvement took place in a large U.S. oil and gas producer and retailer. Several members of the strategy clarification subteam had been involved in the company's strategy-setting process from day one—two of them, in fact, had helped to manage that process—and their experience with the strategy team helped the subteam to manage the clarification process. Moreover, these two members provided valuable insight into the intended goals and requirements of the business strategy.

Many organizations with a multi-business-unit structure will develop both a corporate-wide strategy and separate strategies for each business unit. Business units are usually defined by geography, industry, product line, or some combination of these elements. Accordingly, each business unit's strategy should reflect the uniqueness of its particular situation. However, to achieve resource synergies and leverage and to address the potential white space opportunities that a business unit might miss on its own, a corporate-wide strategy is also needed. Likewise, the business units' strategies should support the corporate-wide strategy so that the overall goals the company has developed will be achieved. Consequently, the strategy clarification subteam needs to understand both the corporate-wide strategy and the strategies of each business unit.

A key outcome of this phase of this subteam's effort is that their work often serves as a catalyst for management to place precedence

Figure 4.2 Typical Making Strategy Work Project Road Map: Strategy Clarification

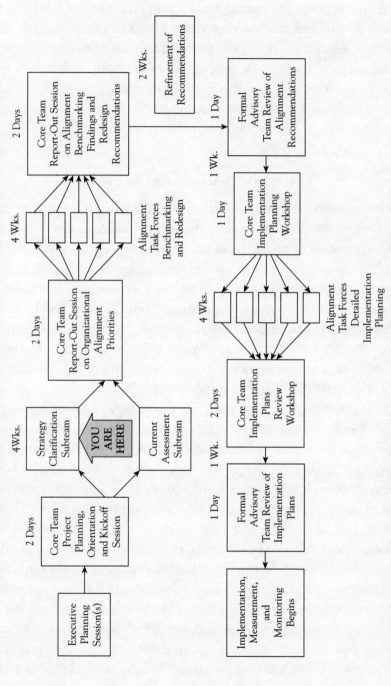

Approximately sixteen weeks from two-day kickoff session to beginning of implementation.

on one aspect of the strategy rather than on others, which helps to address the resource leverage issues noted in Chapters One and Three. Also, the work of the subteam frequently will identify unwanted gaps, overlaps, or deficiencies in the company's or business units' strategies. Finally, this part of the strategy clarification subteam's work is a prerequisite to determining the behaviors and competencies necessary to achieve the business goals of the strategy.

The Strategy Clarification Process

The strategy clarification subteam should approach their effort as a miniproject within the overall strategy implementation endeavor. The members of the subteam need to identify data sources, establish their own milestones, and arrange interview schedules, data analysis formats, and so on. Data sources for the subteam include senior executives from the corporate and business unit levels, managers, employees, and documentation resulting from the strategy development effort. To access all of these sources is unrealistic. However, a good sample can be achieved through selected interviews, focus groups, and/or surveys.

Figure 4.3 provides an example of a strategy clarification matrix that can be used as a survey, interview, or focus group guide or as a template for assessing a company's strategy documentation. The matrix identifies the core elements of a company's strategy, for both corporate-wide and business unit strategies. Additionally, the desired outcomes, business goals, and time frames associated with each strategy, and who is responsible or "owns" the accomplishment of each strategy, should be specified. In addition to using the matrix, the subteam can pose the following prioritization question to help management and employees clarify the critical element or elements of the company's strategy: What will be the driving force or forces of company success over the next five years? Customer satisfaction? Financial stability? Human resources/employees? New products and/or services? Quality improvement? Technological innovations?

Figure 4.3 Sample Strategy Clarification Matrix

Business Unit	Core Elements of Strategy (shrink, grow, harvest, establish a new business, acquire, add new products, etc.)	Desired Outcomes/ Business Goals and Time Frames (establish a new market, grow revenue, enhance profitability, increase market share, etc.)	Responsibility/ Ownership
Corporate-wide			
Unit A			
Unit B			
Unit C			
Unit D			

Operational efficiency? Speed to market? Marketing, advertising, and sales?

Implications of Growth Strategies

As the subteam conducts their strategy clarification work, they need to be cognizant of the difficulties growth strategies present for companies. Awareness of these difficulties will help the clarification subteam, and the entire core team for that matter, build a better description of and plan to develop the competencies and behaviors needed to make the company's growth strategy successful (for example, how to quickly develop competencies in international business or language skills to facilitate a strategy of rapid international expansion). In addition to the difficulties of growth, the subteam should also be aware of the change management challenges associated with growth. Understanding the change management challenges of growth helps the core team address these challenges during implementation planning and accomplishment later in the Making Strategy Work process (for example, how to work short time lines, address communications issues, or contend with the scrutiny of analysts and shareholders). Both the difficulties resulting from growth strategies and the change management challenges associated with them are discussed below.

As noted elsewhere in this book, growth strategies present considerably more challenges to organizations than downsizing strategies do. The challenges created by downsizing include a demoralized workforce, a negative public image, reduced productivity, and so forth. The challenges presented by growth strategies, however, are far greater and farther-reaching.

Many of the headaches of company growth are related to technology, finance, logistics, and operations. Experience shows, however, that most of the problems of growth are created by people-related factors. Galpin and Robinson (1997) state, "In fact, one manager who was overwhelmed by the complexities of her company's fast growth rate commented . . . 'On paper our growth projections look great to analysts and shareholders, but they present people and change management challenges like none I have ever seen. Growth like we have had in the past few years has really raised the bar for our whole management team'" (p. 15).

Growth is intimidating. The growth that takes place in today's organizations is unlike that of the past when planning and implementation activities spanned several years and were mainly sequential. Major expansions—such as a push into a new market, the establishment of overseas locations, creating entirely new manufacturing lines, and so on—were planned for months, phased in over time, and often done in isolation of other initiatives, but this is no longer the case. Today growth initiatives overlap. For example, an acquisition will overlap with expansion into foreign markets, which will overlap with new product launches, and so on. The recovery time that companies once had between when one initiative was planned and implemented and the next initiative came along does not exist any longer. There is no longer time for management and employees alike to catch their breath between initiatives.

In addition technological solutions are being created faster than ever. With the abundant supply of new solutions available, the potential for doing things faster, better, and cheaper can more readily be realized. Accordingly, organizational growth is not only facilitated but is also accelerated by the quickening pace of technological development. Moreover, along with new technology comes a demand for enhanced education and knowledge development.

Growth into foreign markets brings entirely new complexities to an organization. Even simple communication becomes a challenge when organizations are faced with language and time zone obstacles. Differences between countries' cultures can derail even the most well-intentioned activities, and skill sets can vary widely from region to region.

Finally, fast growth creates huge challenges in creating and maintaining organizational competencies. Skilled workers who possess key competencies for growth (such as technology skills, communication and language skills, and management and leadership skills) are becoming harder to come by as the demand for qualified people increases. The issue of competencies will be discussed in more detail in the next chapter.

For these reasons, growth can frighten even seasoned managers. Understanding and addressing the change-management challenges associated with these potential obstacles to growth are just as critical to the success of company expansion as are the formulation and execution of growth strategies themselves. Change-management challenges are, however, neither new nor limited to company growth. Most of the challenges faced during growth are actually encountered in some form or fashion in any organizational change (including restructuring, reengineering, and the like). Unfortunately, during rapid growth, when resources are strained, management often fails to address sound change-management fundamentals. Figure 4.4 lists ten change dynamics that typically come into play during growth. Most growth initiatives contain at least some of each dynamic. Unfortunately, these change dynamics are often overlooked

Figure 4.4 Change Dynamics Brought About by Growth

- Aggressive targets
- Organizational capability demands
- Short time lines
- Communications issues
- Intense scrutiny from analysts and shareholders
- Reengineering of processes
- Cultural fit
- Worker competency requirements
- Politics and positioning
- Large-scale education initiatives

as growth begins, and further ignored as expansion accelerates. But in most cases these dynamics are inevitable, and they can be unforgiving in their impact.

Conclusion

All indications are that growth will be the strategy of choice for many companies into the foreseeable future. Although expansion looks good on paper, the real challenge comes from the people-related issues created by it. Early in the strategy implementation effort, the strategy clarification subteam needs to quickly gain an understanding of the company's strategy, of the priorities the strategy dictates, and of its implications (that is, the necessary competencies, the communications challenges, the training ramifications, the hiring and selection assumptions, and so forth). Once the team has a good understanding of the strategy, it is only half done with its work. The other half of the team's effort is to identify the individual and organizational behaviors and competencies necessary to achieve the aims of the firm's strategy. This part of the subteam's work is addressed in the next chapter.

Chapter Five

Determining the Necessary Competencies and Behaviors

Once the business strategy and its aims are clearly understood, the third stage of the Making Strategy Work project is undertaken: determining the individual and organizational behaviors and competencies that are necessary to achieve the strategy (see Figure 5.1). The strategy clarification subteam described in the previous chapter completes this work (see Figure 5.2).

Focusing on Behaviors in Strategy Implementation

Strategic change occurs at two basic levels within all organizations. At one level are the *values and beliefs* shared by the people in a company. Values and beliefs can be radically different from company to company and from group to group within the same company. For example, one group (such as sales and marketing) may value money and recognition, while another (such as research and development) may value innovation, and yet another (such as human resources and training) may believe that the development of people is of primary importance.

At another level, strategic organizational change occurs in the common *behaviors* of people within a group. Like values and beliefs, behaviors can vary substantially from one group to another. For instance, one group may respond quickly to customer requests, the members of another group may frequently challenge one another's ideas, and a third group may always show up to meetings on time. Behaviors, however, are more tangible than values and beliefs. They can be directly seen and heard (they are visible); values and

**Figure 5.1   The Six Stages of the
Making Strategy Work Project: Stage Three**

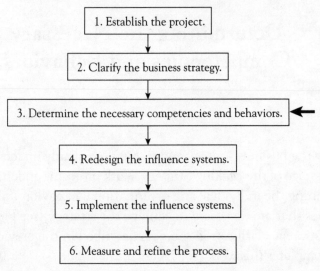

beliefs cannot (they are invisible). They can be directly measured; values and beliefs cannot. And they have a direct impact on operations and business results; values and beliefs do not. Figure 5.3 contrasts these two basic levels of strategic organizational change. Because behaviors are more tangible than values and beliefs, they are easier to change, and facilitating such change should be the essence of strategic implementation efforts. In fact, as John Kotter and James Heskett (1992) state, "In this [behavioral] sense [organizations are] still tough to change, but not nearly as difficult as at the level of basic values" (p. 4).   Other researchers have also written about the importance of focusing on behaviors during strategy implementation efforts. For example, Randy Creek (1995) notes, "Attitudes are personal and private, and cannot be measured. . . . An organization's behavior can be charted, identified and listed" (p. 37). Likewise, Susan Haslett (1995) describes the strategic change process at Fine Products, "a successful, highly profitable consumer products company" (p. 40). She explains that management recognized that the

Figure 5.2 Typical Making Strategy Work Project Road Map: Determining Necessary Competencies and Behaviors

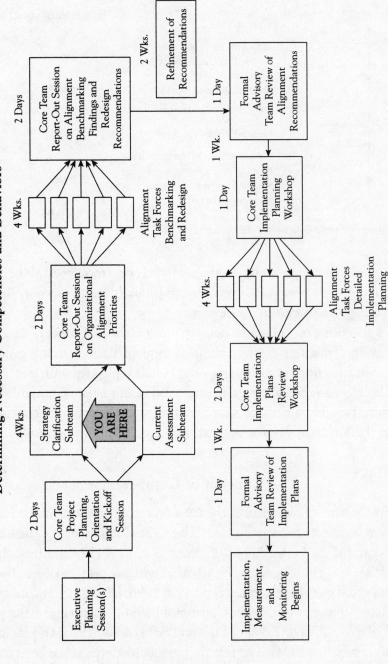

Approximately sixteen weeks from two-day kickoff session to beginning of implementation.

Figure 5.3   The Two Levels of Strategic Organizational Change

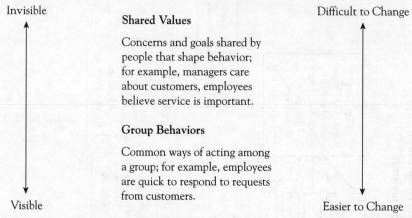

Invisible   Difficult to Change

Shared Values

Concerns and goals shared by
people that shape behavior;
for example, managers care
about customers, employees
believe service is important.

Group Behaviors

Common ways of acting among
a group; for example, employees
are quick to respond to requests
from customers.

Visible   Easier to Change

Source: Adapted from Kotter and Heskett, 1992.

success of change efforts was based largely on employees' ability to change their behaviors, even though their old behaviors may have made them successful in the past.

Focusing on behaviors helps to remove the ambiguity of a strategy implementation effort. Strategy implementation that is geared toward altering people's values and beliefs is plagued with a lack of clarity, vague goals, poor measures, and limited, if any, tangible results. Behaviorally based strategic change efforts are more concrete in their goals, measures, activities, and most important, results.

The Concept of Competencies

At the time of this writing, the most reprinted article from the *Harvard Business Review* is entitled "The Core Competence of the Corporation," by C. K. Prahalad and Gary Hamel (1990). Since that article was published, numerous other writings on the subject have appeared (see, for example, Bordogna, 1996; Du Gay, Salaman, and Rees, 1996; Franzie, 1996; Harrington, 1996; Martin and Behrens, 1996; McDowell, 1996; LeBleu and Sobkowiak, 1995; and Hamel and Prahalad, 1994). The fact that so much attention has been paid to the topic of core competencies indicates that there is a genuine desire on the part of management to take advantage of the concept put forth by Prahalad and Hamel, but many companies have struggled to do so. In fact, Prahalad and Hamel themselves point out the difficulty companies have in even identifying their core competencies. Consequently, before the strategy clarification subteam can identify the competencies that are necessary to achieve the aims of a business strategy, its members need to understand what a core competency is. The difference between behaviors and competencies should be made clear. A *competency* is a process or a collection of *skills; behaviors* are what people regularly say and do to display the competencies they possess. For example, a large retail chain identified sales and customer service as a core competency. The associated behaviors they identified as displaying this competency included smiling while talking to customers, saying hello and thank you, and greeting a customer within thirty seconds of the customer's entering the store.

If the concept of competencies is so confusing, why is there so much interest in them as they relate to strategy implementation? First, identifying competencies provides management with a means of determining the gaps between the skills and capabilities that a company currently possesses and those that it will need in the future. Second, the competencies identified help to determine the individual and team skills required to develop the necessary competencies. Third, describing necessary competencies helps greatly in identifying the priority influence systems that are to be realigned with the strategic needs of the business. Fourth, communicating the necessary competencies helps employees and management to understand how their skills and abilities support the business strategy. Once they understand which competencies are necessary, they can begin to develop them.

Company-Wide Core Competencies

How are company-wide core competencies best defined? Hamel and Prahalad (1994) offer a definition. They contend that for a competency to be considered "core," it must pass three tests: (1) it must add significantly to *customer value*, such as Honda's expertise in engine production or Federal Express's logistics management; (2) it must provide *competitor differentiation*, that is, it must be possessed by the company in a way that is vastly superior to other companies (for example, the customer service competency maintained by Nordstrom); and (3) it must be *extendible* beyond a singular business within a company (for example, the extension of Honda's engine expertise beyond automobiles into motorcycles, lawn tractors, and so on). This three-way definition helps greatly in understanding what a core company-wide competency is. However, there is no cookie-cutter template that management can use to determine a company's core competencies. People need to wrestle with the skills and capabilities resident in their own company to determine which ones they see as really being core. In fact, as Hamel and Prahalad (1994) comment, "As a practical matter, if in defining the core competencies of a medium-sized company or business unit a team of managers comes up with 40, 50, or more 'competencies,' they're probably describing constituent skills and technologies. . . . On the other hand, if they list only one or two competencies, they're probably using too broad a level of aggregation to yield any meaningful insights" (p. 223). Figures 5.4 and 5.5 offer examples of company-wide strategies and competencies identified by two firms during their strategy implementation efforts.

Tiered Competencies

Competencies can exist at levels below that of an entire organization. They can be specific to a business unit, a team, and even an individual.

Business-unit competencies often are similar to company-wide competencies. However, the particular business strategy of a unit may dictate a need for specialized competencies. For example, one business unit in a company may wish to pursue a growth strategy that would create the need to build marketing, sales, and customer service competencies, while another business unit in the same company

Figure 5.4 Strategies and
Associated Competencies of a Propane Retailer

The Company
- Propane retail and propane-related appliances, petroleum refining and marketing, convenience store retail operations
- 1995 revenues: approximately $3 billion
- Employees: 5,100

Growth Strategy
- Transform company from an asset operator into a products and services marketer
- Seek mutually beneficial business alliances
- Heighten customer focus
- Establish operational excellence

Company-Wide Core Competencies Identified
- Marketing expertise
- Leadership skills
- Business development
- Customer service

Figure 5.5 Strategies and Associated Competencies
of a Newspaper Printer/Distributor

The Company
- Newspaper printer and distributor (publishes more than one hundred daily papers in the United States and Canada)
- 1995 revenues: approximately $1.1 billion

Growth Strategy
- Offer more targeted products and services
- Expand products into electronic areas
- Become a marketing company, with newspapers as a core product
- Establish a series of strategic marketing groups in major markets of the United States and Canada

Company-Wide Core Competencies Identified
- Gathering, analyzing, and disseminating news and local information
- Database and electronic services
- Daily, on-time delivery of products to customers
- Linking advertisers with current and potential customers

might wish to pursue a "harvest" strategy, such as maximizing profits with little or no growth, that would produce the need to enhance the financial management competencies across the unit.

At the next level are *team* competencies. These are the skills and capabilities needed within a particular area, such as manufacturing, customer service, finance, marketing, human resources, systems, and so forth. For example, Ronald LeBleu and Roger Sobkowiak (1995) discuss the competencies needed in an information systems (IS) area of a company. They contend that no matter what strategy a company pursues (whether mergers, acquisitions, outsourcing, new markets, or something else) or what technological direction a company takes (such as a client/server system, personal computers, wireless communications, and so forth), IS areas must continually reskill and stay ahead of the curve. LeBleu and Sobkowiak state, "Some companies have already built and are in the process of implementing competency models to guide them in this quest. . . . Many others have it on the drawing board or in their formally approved plans" (p. 7). They propose a competency model based on three core elements: (1) knowledge, (2) skills, and (3) behaviors (for example, IS professionals learn to seek out information needed to complete assignments). Similarly, human resources and finance functions are building more consultative competencies (such as coaching and project management) and moving away from the traditional administrative skills and abilities that have defined these functions for so long. And Joseph Bordogna (1996) identifies new competencies, such as manufacturing science and the application of technology, that are needed in production areas to promote reconfigurable, scaleable, cost-effective manufacturing processes.

At the most granular level are *individual* competencies. Many companies struggle with the vast array of knowledge and skills that can be generated when competency building efforts are focused down to the individual level. Literally hundreds of technical and interpersonal skills can be identified when looking at the individual work done within even one business unit. But developing individual competencies need not be as overwhelming as it first appears.

Rather than delineating specific job skills (which shift all the time), companies are focusing more on *categories* of individual skills and knowledge for various *roles* in a company, business unit, or team. Scott Martin and Gary Behrens (1996), for example, present a senior management competency model based on their evaluation of some four thousand entry-level supervisors, mid-level managers, and senior executives. Through their work they discerned characteristics that are "most likely to distinguish successful executives from entry-level managers" (p. 9): responsibility, creativity, stress tolerance, personal insight, and communication. They contend that excellence in these competencies sets executives apart from other levels of management.

Beyond the executive levels of the organization, Gene Dalton and Paul Thompson (1993) identify a schema of four *career stages:* (1) performing subtasks under supervision; (2) showing distinctive competence (such as contributing individually by accomplishing a part of a project); (3) guiding, developing, and interfacing (for example, serving as a mentor or integrator); and (4) shaping organizational direction (such as serving as director, sponsor, or strategist). Dalton and Thompson suggest that a person must successfully acquire and perform the competencies within each stage before moving into the next stage. Expanding on Dalton's and Thompson's competency categorization, the research division at Watson Wyatt Worldwide (1997) has developed five categories by separating Dalton's and Thompson's second category (showing distinctive competence) into two categories. Their five categories are (1) creating value under direction, (2) creating value independently, (3) creating value through expertise, (4) creating value through others, and (5) creating value through vision.

By employing a focus on categories of competencies that apply to roles within a company, the task of identifying competencies that individuals need becomes vastly more manageable. Utilizing categories also enables a company to focus its resources, coordinate activities, and create a level of consistency in their competency-building efforts that is not afforded when trying to develop specific work skills and abilities.

When determining the behaviors and competencies necessary to support a company's business strategy, the clarification subteam should ask the following key question: What behaviors and competencies will be necessary to successfully achieve the business strategy? Technical? Problem-solving? Interpersonal? Independent judgment and initiative? Leadership? Project management? Communication? General business? Financial? Customer service and sales? Teamwork? Others?

The responses to this question are not sacrosanct to any one group or level. The question can be asked of executives, middle management, and employees. Moreover, the subteam can add to, delete from, and/or modify the list of responses as it determines is necessary. The answers obtained by the subteam should feed into their analyses to determine the behaviors and competencies that, when developed, will support the business strategy.

Conclusion

The work of clarifying the business strategy and determining necessary behaviors and competencies is not easy for the subteam. The task goes more smoothly if a clear business strategy already exists and if thought has been given to the behaviors and competencies that are necessary to successfully pursue the company's strategy. Often, firm-wide competencies have been identified, but business unit, team, and individual competencies have been left ambiguous. Utilizing categories of competencies for the roles within a company can help greatly in identifying individual competencies and in focusing resources on developing them. Finally, frequent changes to the business strategy combined with subsequent revisions of necessary behaviors and competencies only dilutes resources and diminishes the return from strategy implementation efforts. Consistent, focused pursuit of agreed-upon strategies, competencies, and behaviors strengthens resource leverage and helps facilitate the attainment of desired strategic goals.

Chapter Six

Redesigning the Influence Systems

The fourth stage of the Making Strategy Work process is redesigning the influence systems in order to create the necessary competencies and behaviors determined in the third stage (see Figure 6.1).

Assessing the Influence Systems

The first step in the process of redesigning the influence systems is assessing the current state of those systems. While the strategy clarification subteam is conducting its work during the weeks following

Figure 6.1 The Six Stages of the Making Strategy Work Project: Stage Four

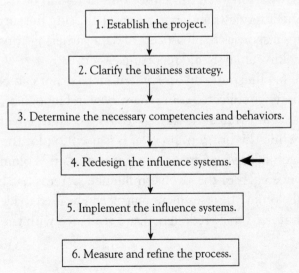

1. Establish the project.

2. Clarify the business strategy.

3. Determine the necessary competencies and behaviors.

4. Redesign the influence systems. ◀

5. Implement the influence systems.

6. Measure and refine the process.

the project kickoff meeting, the other half of the project core team, known as the *current assessment subteam*, performs this evaluation work. Figure 6.2 identifies the milestone on the project road map where this effort occurs.

Like the strategy clarification subteam, the current assessment subteam should approach its effort as a miniproject within the overall strategy deployment endeavor. The members of this subteam also need to identify data sources, establish their own milestones, and arrange interview schedules, data analysis formats, and so on. Data sources for the current assessment subteam include senior executives from the corporate and business unit levels, other managers, and company employees. The current assessment can be done through interviews, focus groups, and/or surveys. A useful survey format that can lend analytical rigor to the assessment of the influence systems is presented in Figure 6.3. The survey can be completed by senior executives, upper and middle management, and/or employees. Furthermore, during data analysis, survey results can be segmented by these groups, by locations, and/or by functional area of the business (such as systems, finance, operations, marketing, and so on). Doing so will provide a broader view of the current state of the systems in various areas of the company, as well as across the entire company. Moreover, the survey questions can be used during one-on-one interviews and in focus groups. Using the survey questions keeps responses to all aspects of data gathering consistent in format, making analysis and reporting easier.

Figure 6.4 illustrates an assessment matrix that can be used to plot the findings collected using the survey in Figure 6.3. The vertical (y) axis illustrates the ratings for the "current effectiveness" column, while the horizontal (x) axis is used to plot the "importance in achieving/supporting the business plan" column of the survey. Once each of the twelve influence systems has been surveyed and plotted, the assessment matrix can be used to identify the systems that need to be redesigned and realigned with the business strategy.

Figure 6.2 Typical Making Strategy Work Project Road Map: Influence Systems Assessment

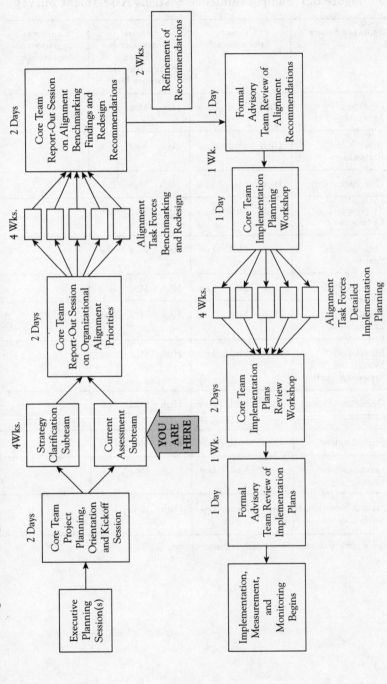

Approximately sixteen weeks from two-day kickoff session to beginning of implementation.

Figure 6.3 Sample Influence Systems Assessment Survey

Influence System	Current Effectiveness*		Future Importance in Achieving/ Supporting the Business Plan*		Comments/ Suggestions for Improvement
Goals and Measures	High Med. Low		High Med. Low		
Rewards and Recognition	High Med. Low		High Med. Low		
Communications	High Med. Low		High Med. Low		
Training and Development	High Med. Low		High Med. Low		
Organizational Structure	High Med. Low		High Med. Low		
Rules and Policies	High Med. Low		High Med. Low		
Physical Environment	High Med. Low		High Med. Low		
Information Systems and Knowledge Sharing	High Med. Low		High Med. Low		
Operational/Process Changes	High Med. Low		High Med. Low		
Senior Leadership	High Med. Low		High Med. Low		
Ceremonies and Events	High Med. Low		High Med. Low		
Staffing, Selection, and Succession	High Med. Low		High Med. Low		

*Please circle your response for each influence system.

Figure 6.4 Current Assessment Summary Matrix

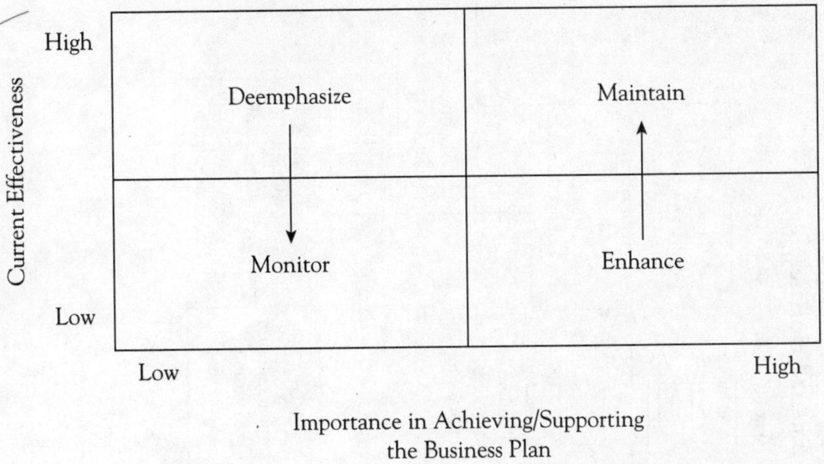

Setting Organizational Alignment Priorities

After completing the survey and the assessment matrix, the two subteams (the strategy clarification subteam and the current assessment subteam) come back together to report out and synthesize their findings, and to determine the *organizational alignment priorities*. This is done in a two-day working session. Figure 6.5 illustrates the point on the project road map where this session occurs. A sample alignment priorities session outline is provided in Appendix B.

The prioritizing of influence systems should be based on the needs created by the business strategy and the current assessment of the influence systems. As demonstrated by the case examples presented in Chapter Two, each company will realign different influence systems to support their strategies. Moreover, as the research and case examples in Chapter Two illustrate, there exists no clear empirical evidence of which influence systems have the greatest impact on creating necessary behaviors and competencies or desired business results. At the very least, companies should be aligning their goals and measures, rewards and recognition, training and development, communications, senior leadership, and ceremonies

Figure 6.5 Typical Making Strategy Work Project Road Map: Report-Out Session on Organizational Alignment Priorities

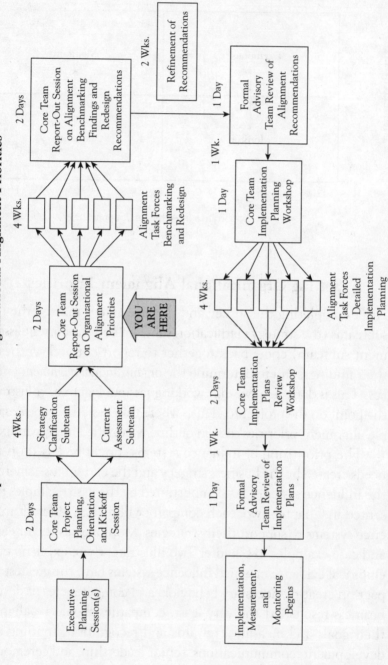

Approximately sixteen weeks from two-day kickoff session to beginning of implementation.

and events influence systems with their business strategy. That is not to say that the other systems are not as important. Again, more research is needed to identify the influence systems, or combinations of them, that have the maximum impact on deploying a company's strategy.

Alignment Task Forces

After the priority influence systems have been selected by the core team during their two-day session, the redesign of the influence systems should be coordinated by the project core team, but the actual redesign work is most effectively done by a series of *strategic alignment task forces* (ATFs) reporting to the core team. As described in Chapter Three, the ATFs are actually led by members of the core team. However, other members of the organization should be involved at this stage to round out the membership of the task forces and to assist with the redesign and subsequent implementation efforts.

Once they are established, the ATFs should be oriented to the Making Strategy Work project, to the work they need to perform, to the products they are expected to produce, and to the time line on which they will be working. This orientation is most effectively done through the use of *task force charters* (see Figure 6.6). Each charter should be developed by the core team member who is selected to lead the task force. It should then be reviewed with the project manager and ultimately shared with the task force in their first meeting.

Figure 6.7 presents ten ATF work steps, along with resulting outputs, that can be used to augment each task force charter. In addition, Appendix C presents an alignment task forces guidebook that includes the charter template and the ten task force steps. The guidebook can be used to orient the task force members during their first meeting, and it can act as a valuable resource tool for each task force during its planning and implementation work.

Figure 6.6 Task Force Charter Template

Task Force Name: _____

Members: _____ *Leader(s)

_____

_____

_____

_____

_____

Task Force Goals/Deliverables (including due dates):

Reporting/Communication (accountability to whom and how often):

Resource(s) (needs and availability):

Links to Other Task Forces (for cross–task force integration):

Figure 6.7 Ten Alignment Task Force Work Steps

Step One	A: Detail current practices O: Basic understanding of the current influence system	Where are we?
Step Two	A: Conduct benchmarking and best practices O: Comparison with other companies	How do we compare?
Step Three	A: Develop redesign recommendations O: Initial realignment designs	Where are we going?
Step Four	A: Integrate various task force recommendations O: Integrated recommendations	Are we coordinated?
Step Five	A: Gain redesign approval O: Advisory team approval of redesign recommendations	Are we in agreement?
Step Six	A: Develop detailed implementation plans O: Announcements, training materials, logistics, scheduling, and so forth	Are we ready?
Step Seven	A: Gain implementation approval O: Advisory team go-ahead approval	Can we implement?
Step Eight	A: Implement O: Conduct training, make announcements, and so forth	Go
Step Nine	A: Measure, monitor, and adjust O: Process reports, process adjustments	Course corrections
Step Ten	A: Completion O: Disband task forces and celebration	Finish

LEGEND: A = Action
O = Output

Cross–Task Force Communication and Coordination

As the ATFs do their work, overlaps, gaps, and integration issues will frequently arise among the groups throughout the process, because each task force addresses issues that affect the other task forces as well as their own. Consequently, a solid cross–task force communication process should be established. The communication process among the task forces should also address the systemic nature of the influence systems and facilitate the integrated approach to realigning them. Consider the following example.

In a large Canadian insurance company, several task forces were established to work on realigning the influence systems with the company's growth strategy, including compensation, training, communications, organization structure, and so on. As each task force worked in its own area, they all kept their focus on the broader integration issues of consistency and overlap among the various influence systems. This focus was accomplished by three key mechanisms. First, each ATF leader was required to submit to the project manager every Friday a one-page weekly progress summary. The summary template was designed for the task force leaders to use bullet format reporting, and took only twenty to thirty minutes to complete each week (see Figure 6.8).

Second, the leaders of the ATFs (who were the members of the project's core team) met every Monday morning for two hours to report on the previous week's progress and identify issues of overlap among the task forces. The core team's leader (the project manager) ran the meetings, and each task force leader gave a brief ten-minute report on key highlights of their task force's progress during the previous week. As overlaps or gaps were identified during the meeting, the project manager recorded them on a flipchart. The core team did not try to solve any of the overlap issues in the plenary session. Once the overlap issues list was completed, the task forces that needed to be involved in resolving those issues were assigned to address them. Any particular issue could involve two, three, or more task forces. It was then the job of each task force leader to meet with the other

Figure 6.8 Alignment Task Force
Weekly Progress Summary Template

(Used by each task force to update the project manager
at the end of every week about the team's progress.)

Task force name:

Week ending:

1. Key actions during the past week:

2. Key successes:

3a. Key issues:

3b. Potential solutions/help needed:

4. Next steps/actions:

5. Other key information:

leaders assigned to the same issue and work out solutions by the next core team plenary meeting. In the event that the few task force leaders remained at an impasse, they brought their solution options and supporting rationales to the next core team meeting for the whole group to consider. If the core team could not decide on the best solution for the overlap issue, the issue was taken to the project sponsor, who would act as the tie breaker. Over a four-month period, the project sponsor needed to function as the tie breaker only once.

The third cross-team communication mechanism required each task force to identify early in their formation the other task forces with which they would need to stay coordinated throughout the re-design process. Once the task forces had made their lists, each team assigned a liaison to work with each of the other task forces identi-fied on their coordination list. This often required the designated liaisons to participate in other task forces' working meetings. For ex-ample, the systems task force needed to coordinate with several other task forces, including training, hiring and selection, compen-sation, and so on. Consequently, a person from the systems task force participated in each of the other task force meetings and brought back pertinent information for the systems task force to address.

By incorporating these three project coordination and integra-tion mechanisms, the insurance company's ability to grapple with the systemic interaction of the influence systems was greatly enhanced.

Conclusion

The task forces' first step (see Figure 6.7) is to detail the current prac-tices of the influence system to which they have been assigned. This detailing is done at a deeper, more specific level than the initial as-sessment conducted by the current assessment subteam. However, the task forces can use the output of the subteam's initial assessment as a starting point for their work. The details that the task forces should work to delineate at this point can include (1) the steps involved in performing the influence system; (2) the roles performed by line management, employees, and others (such as human re-sources, finance, and so on); (3) the variations in the influence system throughout the company (by geography or operating unit); (4) the costs involved; (5) the time the influence system currently takes; and so on. The main goal of this step is for each task force to develop quickly a good picture of the current makeup and impact of the influence system they are redesigning, before moving on to the next step—conducting benchmarking and best practices—which is discussed in the next chapter.

Chapter Seven

Comparing Yourself to Others

The second step in the alignment task forces' (ATFs') redesign and implementation efforts (see Figure 6.7) involves the use of two valuable tools: *benchmarking* and *best practices*. These activities are conducted after a task force has detailed the current practices of the influence system on which they are working. Figure 7.1 illustrates the point on the Making Strategy Work road map at which benchmarking and best practices activity occurs.

Benchmarking or Best Practices?

Some may think it is splitting hairs, but there is a difference between the terms *benchmarking* and *best practices*, and in many organizations there is a lot of confusion over the difference. The key dissimilarity is in the type of data that is collected by or exchanged between companies. The data for benchmarking is typically quantitative (such as number of employees, cost per employee, revenue per employee, and so on), whereas the data for best practices is typically qualitative (such as how a company rewards its people, why they use the structure they do, the steps they take in a process, and so forth). This simple distinction can help to ease the definition arguments that often occur in companies, which too frequently divert attention away from the main purposes of the activity: to see how one company stacks up against another and to obtain innovative ideas.

What is a best practice and how is it determined? The determination of a best practice is often based on the observer's point of view. Some of the ambiguity of this approach can be alleviated,

Figure 7.1 Typical Making Strategy Work Project Road Map: Benchmarking and Best Practices

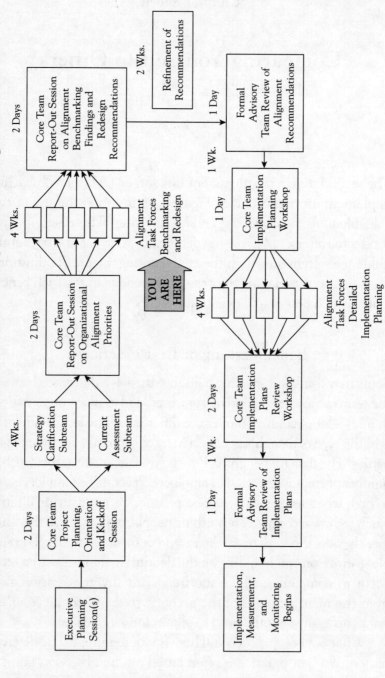

Approximately sixteen weeks from two-day kickoff session to beginning of implementation.

however, by identifying criteria for calling a process or a company a best practice. People Management Resources, located in Beaverton, Oregon, maintains a database of best practices in human resources management areas, including employee communications, recognition, leadership development and succession planning, performance measurement, staffing and selection, and training. Their data cover more than 450 companies in thirty industries. Their criteria for classifying a company as a best practice is whether or not the company's human resources practices have had a positive impact on financial performance, customer satisfaction, and employee satisfaction. They may also include a company as a best practice if its practices are innovative and progressive, even though the jury may still be out on whether those practices are making a positive impact on performance and/or satisfaction.

Many companies have been using benchmarking as a tool for several years. In a 1992 *Human Resources Executive* special report entitled "Borrowing from the Best: How to Benchmark World-Class People Practices," John Hooper asserts that in 1985 only a small portion of Fortune 500 companies took part in benchmarking (mainly due to the advent of the total quality movement at that time), but by 1990 more than half of these companies were involved in benchmarking. Companies such as Xerox, Motorola, Florida Power & Light, and Ford Motor Company, just to name a few, all have recognized that technology, operational and management innovations, and competition are not stagnant. They use benchmarking as a means not only to stay abreast of new developments but also to leapfrog their competitors. By learning from the trials and tribulations that others have encountered during the development and implementation of, say, a new pay-for-performance system or a new organizational structure, companies can ease their own implementation efforts and often surpass others by avoiding the mistakes they have made. Hooper also notes that smaller companies, such as Sara Lee, Baylor Health Care Systems, and Manco Inc., are also participating in benchmarking on a regular basis.

The Basic Steps of
Benchmarking and Best Practices

There are several steps that, when followed, will make a benchmarking and best practices effort go smoothly. The basic steps of benchmarking and best practices are as follows:

1. *Identify the aspects of the influence system that the task force would like to benchmark.* For example, one company was interested in learning about three key aspects of rewards and recognition: (a) the decision-making process used by other companies to set their compensation and benefits strategy, (b) the ways in which the benchmarked companies used pay and benefits to implement their strategies, and (c) the other rewards and recognition that the companies used in addition to pay and benefits.

2. *Select companies to benchmark.* Select a reasonable number of companies to benchmark. Typically, five to seven companies is a good number. Selecting too many will cost too much time, and selecting too few will not provide a good array of information. Conducting phone interviews rather than site visits is a good way to enable the team to include more companies. Going outside of your industry is often a good way to learn innovative ideas. The types of companies to benchmark include (a) successful competitors, (b) high-performing companies of different sizes and from various industries, and (c) companies receiving notoriety as being innovators.

3. *Design a benchmark interview guide.* An interview guide helps to keep the conversation with a company focused and on track. Additionally, the information collected will be in a consistent format from company to company, facilitating easier data comparison and analysis. Figure 7.2 presents a sample interview guide used by a selection, staffing, and succession ATF.

4. *Contact companies to schedule the interviews.* Schedule the interview with a company representative. Let the task force members know the date and time of the interview so they can schedule

Figure 7.2 Sample Benchmarking Interview Guide

Company: _____

Contact Name and Title: _____

Telephone Number: _____

Date of Interview: _____

Interviewers: _____

Selection and Staffing:

• What practices have you put in place to align your recruiting practices with the strategy of the company?

• How are skills, experience, and education requirements determined? By whom?

• How are internal candidates considered for openings in comparison to external candidates?

• What role does line management play in selection and hiring? Human resources?

• What if any training/orientation do new employees receive? How soon after hiring?

• Describe the steps in your selection and hiring process.

• How do you measure the effectiveness of your selection and hiring process?

Succession:

• Do you have a formal succession planning process?

• How far down in the organizational structure does your succession process go?

• What role does line management play in succession planning? Human resources?

• Describe the steps in your succession planning process.

• How do you measure the effectiveness of your succession planning process?

Any Other Comments:

---

themselves to attend. Not all task force members need to attend each interview.

5. *Send the interview guide to the benchmarked company contacts.* Sending the interview guide to the company contacts ahead of time will help them to prepare their answers. This will facilitate a more focused and effective discussion when the interview is conducted.

6. *Conduct the interview.* Generally, one person from the task force should take the lead during the interview. Others can ask

questions for clarification as needed, but this should not be done too often, because it can sidetrack the conversation and confuse the person or persons being interviewed. Use the interview guide that was sent to the company contact. At the end of the call, thank the contact for her time, remind her that she will get a copy of the results summary, and ask whether it would be all right to call back later if the task force needs to clarify any information they gathered (such follow-up calls are not uncommon).

7. *Summarize the findings.* Summarizing the information gathered from each interview will help the team sort through the information to get a good overview of the benchmarking and best practices findings. Figure 7.3 illustrates a portion of a sample benchmarking and best practices summary matrix for training and development. Using this type of summary helps the task forces begin to develop their redesign ideas.

Avoiding Benchmarking and Best Practices Pitfalls

On the surface, benchmarking and best practices comparisons appear to be relatively simple, but they can quickly get complex and overwhelming, which often leads to ATFs getting discouraged and even giving up on the activities. Recognizing the potential pitfalls of benchmarking and best practices at the start helps task forces to avoid them along the way. First, they will not provide a task force with the silver-bullet answer to its redesign work. Too often, members of a task force will conduct a benchmarking and/or best practices interview and come away saying something like, "We thought they were the best in the world at pay for performance, but we didn't learn anything new." People must take a realistic view, that is, that benchmarking and best practices will provide *ideas, but not necessarily answers.*

Second, be careful not to assume there is an apples-to-apples comparison. For example, a task force wants to compare the cost of an influence system, such as training and development, in one company with that of other companies. When they obtain their

Figure 7.3 Sample Summary Matrix for Benchmarking and Best Practices Interviews

Summary of Other Companies' Practices	Companies Applying Practices	Our Company's Current Practices	Future Implications for Our Company	Rationale
1. Individuals are responsible for their own career development	Company A Company B Company C Company X Company Y Company Z	Employees expect managers to be responsible	Communicate the expectation of employee responsibility for their own development, but provide support mechanisms (such as training, counseling from management about career choices, etc.)	• Creates a better match of employee skills and interests with the job
2. Delivery of training by management is an honor	Company B Company C Company Z	Viewed as an imposition on management	Management at all levels measured and rewarded for delivery of training	• Management continues to learn • Sets an example for employees • Employees strive for their chance to become instructors of the future
3. Participation in core company courses is required	Company A Company B Company Y Company Z	No company-wide core courses exist	Establish company core courses required at various points during a person's career (such as new employee)	• Establishes consistency of company training at various points during career development

quantitative data, the task force finds that there are wild variations in cost per employee. However, they have not gotten beneath the veneer of the training and development systems in the comparison companies to try to understand what actually drives the cost numbers they were given. Do the companies include technical training? Do they include travel costs? Do they include the cost of time off the job? Does on-the-job training count? And so forth. Not getting the whole picture can quickly lead a task force astray.

A third pitfall is trying to be too precise. This can apply to both quantitative and qualitative information. For example, one task force wanted to benchmark the goals and measures influence system of other companies that were pursuing a customer service improvement strategy. They gathered data about how goals and measures were set and about the results of actual measures for the benchmarked companies. The information was good, but the task force started to split hairs within the information. To detect an impact on sales, their analysis broke down the numerical data in various ways, including sales per employee, sales per week, sales per month, customer satisfaction ratings, and others. They also broke down the qualitative (best practices) information into the goal-setting process steps that each company took, how long each step lasted, who was involved, and so on. What the task force lost sight of was the bigger picture they originally wanted to get. Their primary question was, What customer service goals and measures do best practice companies set, and how do they set them? Their intense data analysis led to endless hours of additional work. Moreover, the team was so caught up in doing the correct analysis that they never began looking at what they could glean from their information to use in redesigning their own company's service goals and measures. The message is that directional order of magnitude (the general size of the gap between two or more organizations' practices) rather than detailed precision is the best measure of change.

Fourth, benchmarking and best practices can become expensive and time-consuming. However, they need not be either. Many companies believe that traveling to a company to conduct a site visit is the way to do comparisons. Yet most good benchmarking and best practices information can be gathered over the phone in about an hour. The advantage of phone interviews is that companies are more willing to take part because it is easier, the conversation is more focused, and more people from the task force can participate via speaker phone. Traveling to conduct site visits should be extraordinary, and should have sound justification. Site visits can be expensive and take much more time than a telephone interview.

Fifth, don't get caught up in only comparing your company to others in your own industry or companies that are the same size as your own. Good ideas can come from various places. Pay for performance, communications, training, the use of technology and information sharing, and the like are all being addressed in companies of all sizes and in all industries.

Sixth, not being organized in your approach will quickly derail a benchmarking and best practices effort. Getting a company on the phone but having no predetermined questions or agenda wastes the time of everyone involved from both companies. Another aspect of staying organized is to be sure that no more than one of the task forces contacts the same person from the comparison company. Failure to coordinate the work of the ATFs in this area will only make the company that is doing the benchmarking and best practices look disorganized and poorly managed. The left hand should know what the right hand is doing. Figure 7.4 illustrates a coordination matrix that can be used by the project manager to organize the comparison contacts by the various task forces. The matrix should be posted where all task forces can access it. Using this simple approach will help to coordinate interviews and avoid "going to the well" once too often.

The seventh common pitfall is to approach benchmarking and best practices as an all-take and no-give activity. Offering to share the results of the comparison effort with the companies you approach to benchmark is essential. Sharing the information is a good way not only to say thank you after the benchmarking activity, but

**Figure 7.4 Sample Benchmarking
and Best Practices Coordination Matrix**

Benchmarked Company	Benchmarked Company Contact Person	Task Forces Wanting to Contact	Date for Scheduled Interview
Company X	• Bob J. • Mary R. • Bob J.	• Training • Rewards • Communications	• 11/10 • 11/11 • 11/10
Company Y	• James S. • Pete W. • Peter M.	• Training • Organizational structure • Knowledge sharing	• 11/12 • 11/13 • 11/14
Company Z	• Susan P. • Pam G. • Bill H.	• Training • Communications • Knowledge sharing	• 11/11 • 11/17 • 11/13

also to entice companies to participate in the benchmarking and best practices in the first place. Furthermore, include your own company's information during interviews and in the summary you share with participating companies.

Finally, ensure that there is confidentiality for the benchmark and best practices participants. Often companies are reluctant to participate because they do not want their inside information to become widely publicized. Maintaining confidentiality will avoid potential problems later on.

These guidelines will help to ensure that a benchmarking and best practices effort will run smoothly, and that the information gathered will be useful. Figure 7.5 presents a summary of the general dos and don'ts of benchmarking and best practices.

Alternative Sources of Information

In addition to phone interviews and site visits, there are other ways to obtain benchmarking and best practices information that can broaden the information gathered and/or shorten the cycle time for gaining knowledge. First, publications such as professional journals

Figure 7.5 Benchmarking and Best Practices Dos and Don'ts

Do	Don't
Be organized (preset questions, coordinate interviews between task forces).	Be haphazard.
Look for ideas.	Look for magic solutions.
Understand the differences between companies.	Assume that the information can be compared as "apples to apples."
Conduct telephone interviews, with site visits being extraordinary.	Let benchmarking get too expensive and time-consuming by doing many site visits.
Share information with participating companies.	Just take information and not give any.
Look beyond your company size and industry sector.	Get caught up in your own size and industry.
Ensure confidentiality.	Breech a company's confidentiality.
Look for directional trends and order of magnitude.	Try to get the data too precise.

and magazines often contain good descriptive details of innovative company practices with respect to the various influence systems. Second, management and employees internal to your company can be good sources of information. These people include the sales force, manufacturing personnel, heads of functions and departments, and employees who used to work at other companies. Third, conferences and other professional gatherings can be a good source of learning about innovative practices from various companies. Finally, *Best Practices Resource Guides* detailing numerous companies' practices in many of the influence systems (including employee communications, rewards, staffing and selection, and training) are available from People Management Resources, 14780 Osprey Drive, Suite 275, Beaverton, Oregon, 97007.

Conclusion

Benchmarking and best practices comparisons are some of the best ways to stimulate ideas and expand the task force's thinking about possible alternatives for redesigning the influence systems. Beyond the use of benchmarking and best practices by the ATFs, the information gathered can be presented to the advisory team and others within the organization to help expand their view of the possibilities for redesign. Remember, precision is not the goal. Rather, efficient data collection and synthesis and enhancing the innovative thought of the task forces and others within the organization should be the focus of any benchmarking and best practices activity. Good benchmarking and best practices information will help facilitate the task force's redesign efforts described in the next chapter.

Chapter Eight

Developing Redesign Recommendations and Implementing the Redesigned Influence Systems

The next milestones in the Making Strategy Work project are, first, developing the redesign recommendations, and then, implementing them.

Developing the Redesign Recommendations

The third step (see Figure 6.7) for the Alignment Task Forces (ATFs) is to develop influence system redesign recommendations. (Figure 8.1 indicates the point on the Making Strategy Work project road map where this activity occurs.) There is no magic solution to redesign. Although best practice and benchmarking information provides creative ideas to the task forces, the practices of other companies cannot be copied to the letter. There are too many differences between one company and another. Even between companies in the same industry and of similar sizes there are structural differences, leadership differences, strategy differences, and so on. These differences necessitate that the influence systems be redesigned on the basis of a particular company's unique situation. To help stir up ideas, the ATFs should use the current assessment information gathered by the core team, the details on the current influence systems compiled by the task forces, and the benchmarking information that the task forces have collected.

There are five key questions that ATF members need to ask themselves when generating redesign recommendations:

Figure 8.1 Typical Making Strategy Work Project Road Map: Developing Redesign Recommendations

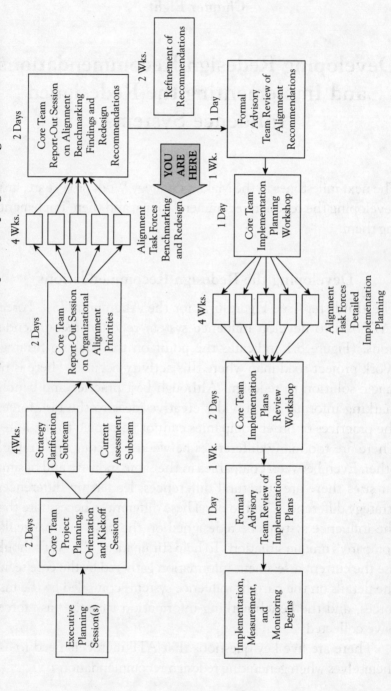

Approximately sixteen weeks from two-day kickoff session to beginning of implementation.

1. *What can we learn from the feedback the organization gave during the current assessment of this system?* The comments that management and employees give during the assessment of current system practices (see Figure 6.3) often provide good ideas for redesign of the influence system.

2. *What did we find when we detailed the current practices of the influence system?* Looking at the detail within an influence system often reveals problems such as misalignment with the business plan, unneeded complexity, unwanted variations throughout the organization, and undesired roles of management, employees, and others.

3. *What can we learn from the best practice companies we talked to?* The answers to this question give insight into what might be possible in the areas of performance, implementation, and measurement of the influence system on which the task force is working.

4. *What key enablers are needed to implement our recommendations?* Enablers include such things as new technology, training, communications, hiring, measures, and so on. Even though these are influence systems themselves, they are often needed as enablers to facilitate the effective implementation of a redesigned influence system.

5. *What impact does the redesign have on the other influence systems?* This question addresses the systemic nature of the influence systems. Redesigning one system often affects the others. Once a task force has identified other influence systems that will be affected by its recommendations, it should keep all of the task forces that are responsible for those influence systems informed about the content of the recommendations.

A good example of answers to these questions comes from a task force in a large oil company working on the redesign of the company's selection and hiring influence system. The task force based its redesign on feedback from employees and management, on the details of the company's current selection and hiring practices, and on the benchmarking information the task force collected. The task force designed a new selection and staffing system that would support the company's strategy of entering into overseas markets in which they had not previously operated. The core competencies necessary to support the strategy were international work capability, and oil and gas exploration and production expertise. The task force found that the company's current hiring system varied widely between business units and did not encourage the movement of qualified internal candidates between the various units of the company (the company had more than forty thousand employees worldwide). The task force designed a hiring and selection system that created consistency throughout the company, and that would facilitate the advertising of positions internally and the nomination of internal candidates. The enablers necessary to realizing the new system included new technology, the training of line management, and communications to all employees. The redesigned selection and hiring system resulted in a number of internal candidates applying for international positions who possessed international work experience as well as exploration and/or production experience. Moreover, the new system reduced the time of hiring by more than a month, enabling the company to pursue its push into the overseas markets on schedule.

Conducting a Recommendations Review Session

Once the ATFs have conducted their benchmarking and redesign work, their fourth step (see Figure 6.7) is to integrate the recommendations of the various task forces. To accomplish this, the task force leaders come together as the project core team to conduct a two-day session on benchmarking findings and redesign recommendations (see Figure 8.2). The purpose of the session is for the task force leaders to (1) report out a summary of their benchmarking findings, (2) compare the task forces' redesign recommendations, and (3) prioritize and integrate the task forces' recommendations. Although the ATFs should have been keeping each other informed up to this point, the recommendations session is designed to enable all of the task force leaders to see the recommendations in total. This

Figure 8.2 Typical Making Strategy Work Project Road Map:
Report-Out Session on Benchmarking Findings and Redesign Recommendations

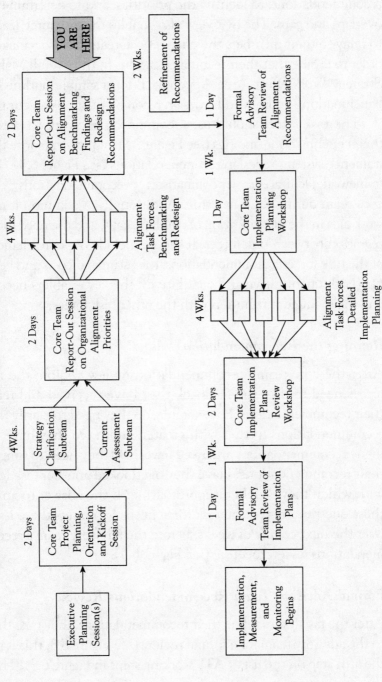

Approximately sixteen weeks from two-day kickoff session to beginning of implementation.

overview helps the core team to assess the cumulative effect of the recommendations, to identify the priorities, and to determine the overlaps and gaps. The overview also enables the task force leaders to relay to their members the changes the team needs to make in order to ensure that their recommendations fit the overall Making Strategy Work effort. (See Appendix B for a sample outline of a benchmarking findings and redesign recommendations meeting.)

The task forces should use a common framework to present their benchmarking findings (see Figure 7.3) and to summarize their influence systems redesign recommendations (see Figure 8.3). This framework facilitates easier comparison of recommendations by the core team during their meeting. Additionally, a common framework aids in the identification of overlaps, gaps, and the need for integration between task forces. It should include the core elements of the task forces' recommendations, the estimated costs and benefits (both quantitative and qualitative), the key enablers needed, and the required integration with the other task forces.

Refining the Recommendations

After the core team's recommendation review session, the task forces need to take the feedback they have received and refine their recommendations. For example, do they need to clarify their recommendations further with greater detail? Do they have too many recommendations and need fewer? Do they need to simplify their recommendations? Have they overlooked another task force with which they should be coordinating? If the answer to any of these questions is yes, the task force needs to address these issues over the next couple of weeks, before the advisory team's recommendations review meeting (see Figure 8.4).

Formal Advisory Team Recommendations Review

After the task forces refine their recommendations, they take them to the advisory team for a formal review (see Figure 8.5; this is also the fifth step on the list of ATF working steps in Figure 6.7). There

Figure 8.3 Sample Task Force Recommendation Template: Hiring and Selection

Recommendation	Estimated Cost/Benefit	Key Enablers	Integration Needed with Other Task Forces
Company-wide job posting	Estimated costs: • $x for automated job-posting system • $y for management training Benefits: • Faster hiring • More qualified candidates identified, possessing needed competencies • Broader job opportunities leading to comprehensive skill development and greater commitment of employees	• Automated job-posting system • Management training to use posting system • Employee communications regarding posting system	• Systems • Training • Communication
Company-wide recruiting services	Estimated costs: • $x for automated job-posting system (same as above) • $y for management training (same as above) Benefits: • Faster hiring • More qualified candidates identified, possessing needed competencies • $z savings due to line management and HR function time reduction/reallocation	• Automated job-posting system • Management training on use of recruiting services	• Systems • Training • Communication

Figure 8.4 Typical Making Strategy Work Project Road Map: Refinement of Recommendations

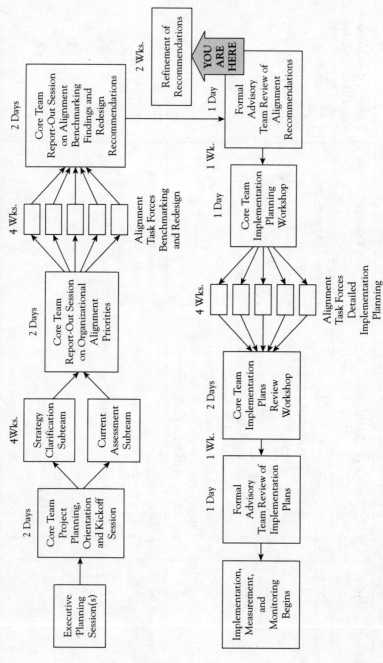

Approximately sixteen weeks from two-day kickoff session to beginning of implementation.

Figure 8.5 Typical Making Strategy Work Project Road Map: Advisory Team Review of Alignment Recommendations

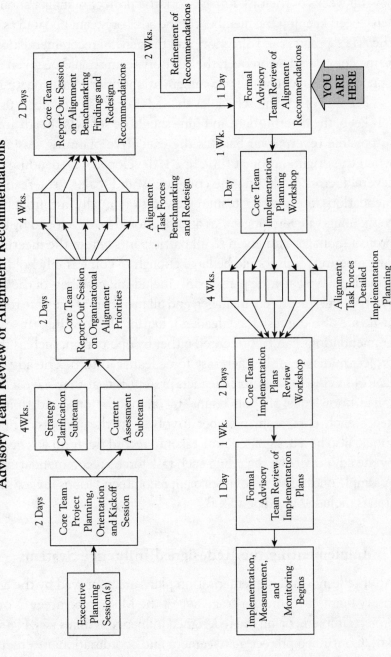

Approximately sixteen weeks from two-day kickoff session to beginning of implementation.

should be no surprises during this meeting. Throughout the past several weeks of the task forces' work the project manager should have been keeping the members of the advisory team updated as to the ATFs' progress and direction, and the general recommendations being considered. Moreover, the advisory team should be given an opportunity to review the recommendations prior to the meeting.

Because of the full schedules that advisory team members usually keep, the meeting date and time should be set as far in advance as possible (even as far back as the executive planning sessions, when the original project time line is developed). Depending on several factors, including the complexity and scale of the recommendations, the advisory team review session usually lasts from two to six hours or even longer. An agenda should be developed by the project manager and given to all participants before the meeting. The meeting room should be large enough to comfortably hold all attendees. Typically the participants include all members of the advisory team, the project manager, and all members of the core team (who are also the task force leaders). During the meeting, the recommendations can be presented either by one person, such as the project manager, or by each task force leader in turn. The advantage of having the task force leaders present is that they have a detailed knowledge of their teams' recommendations, and that it keeps each core team member involved in the process. There should also be a designated note taker to record the feedback given by the advisory team regarding each task force's recommendations. A sample outline of an advisory team recommendations review session is included in Appendix B.

Implementing the Redesigned Influence Systems

After redesign and implementation plans are approved by the advisory team, it is time for stage five of the Making Strategy Work project: implementing the redesigned influence systems (see Figure 8.6). Continued project management and coordination are crucial during implementation because many people beyond the project's

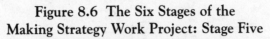

Figure 8.6 The Six Stages of the
Making Strategy Work Project: Stage Five

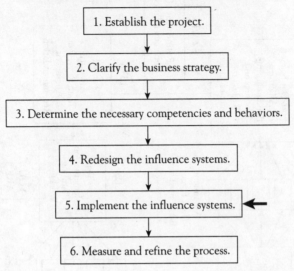

1. Establish the project.

2. Clarify the business strategy.

3. Determine the necessary competencies and behaviors.

4. Redesign the influence systems.

5. Implement the influence systems.

6. Measure and refine the process.

core team and task forces must participate. A cadre of senior executives, managers, and employees should all be involved in delivering communications, conducting training, applying new goals and measures, and so on.

Conducting an Implementation Planning Workshop

After the advisory team review session, the core team should conduct an implementation planning workshop (see Figure 8.7) that includes all of the members of the core team. This workshop is valuable for several reasons. First, the core team members have a chance to debrief each other on the feedback they received from the advisory team review session. Second, the core team members can coordinate implementation priorities based on that feedback. For example, some task force recommendations may be seen by the advisory team as more important than others and need to be given more priority during implementation. Third, the project manager

Figure 8.7 Typical Making Strategy Work Project Road Map: Implementation Planning Workshop

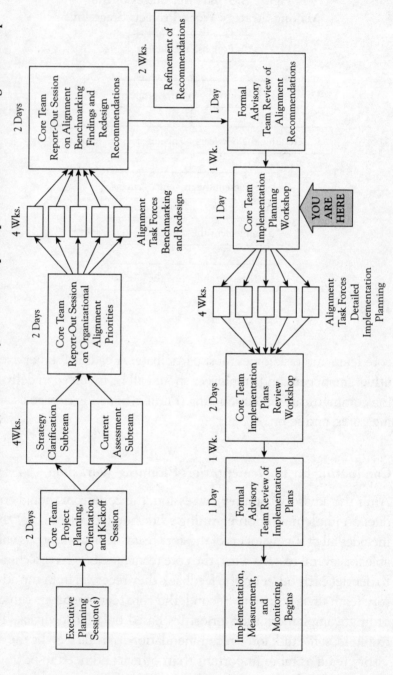

can ensure that each task force understands the time line and the deliverables that are due. Fourth, after the advisory team review meeting, the project manager should update the communication strategy (see Figure 3.5) to prepare for the next wave of communications. Typically, at this stage of the project the communication message is "This is the direction we are taking." The revised communication strategy can be reviewed with the core team members during the implementation workshop. See Appendix B for a sample implementation planning workshop outline.

Detailed Implementation Planning

After the core team conducts its implementation planning workshop, detailed implementation plans should be drafted by each ATF (the sixth step in the ATF working steps listed in Figure 6.7). These plans should include numerous logistical elements, such as timing, training needs, where training will occur, who should attend, how people will be notified, who will conduct the training, what the content will be, and so forth. Additional logistical considerations can include equipment ordering and installation, and facilities planning. Communications is another component that needs to be well planned and executed at this point. Finally, measurement should be included in the implementation plans. A sample detailed implementation planning template is included in the last section of the ATF guidebook in Appendix C. Using this template, each task force can detail the areas of implementation that need to be addressed to ensure timely and effective rollout.

Depending on the project schedule, the task forces typically have approximately four weeks to complete their detailed plans (see Figure 8.8). Again, interaction and cross–task force communication during this period are critical to ensure that overlaps, gaps, and integration are addressed. Therefore, the weekly update summary sheets should still be used, and Monday morning task force leaders' meetings should still occur.

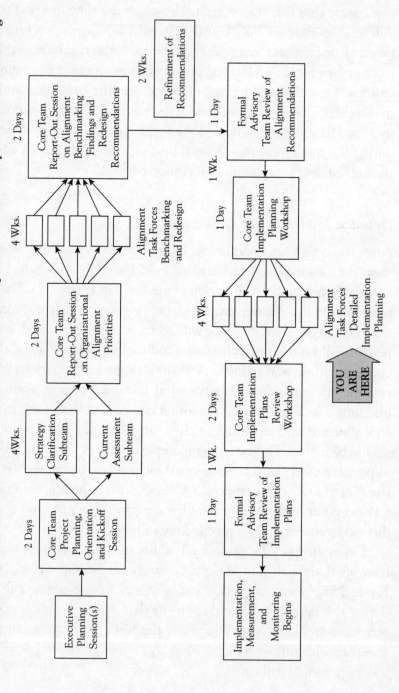

Figure 8.8 Typical Making Strategy Work Project Road Map: ATF Detailed Implementation Planning

Implementation Considerations

As they consider their implementation alternatives, the task forces need to identify the complexities involved in implementation. First, implementation complexity increases when a task force redesigns both the process and the technology of an influence system (see Figure 8.9). The people who must change their behavior and operate an influence system differently need to learn more than just changes to the steps of a process. For example, the management of a large oil company not only had to learn new staffing procedures but also had to change the way employees were sourced and hired. The company put in place an on-line job-posting system that allowed management to more efficiently source internal candidates. However, managers not only needed to learn how to use the new system, they also had to break their old habit of placing an outside ad for external candidates as their first candidate sourcing action. To accomplish these changes, managers received training on using the posting system. Additionally, they could not get an advertisement placed for an external candidate until they had posted an opening internally. The result was a marked increase in the number

Figure 8.9 Degree of Implementation Complexity

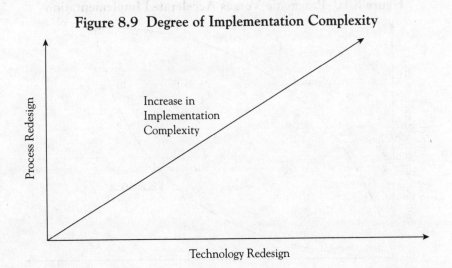

of internal hires, which took much less time than external hires. The new process also had the additional impact of increasing employee development opportunities as it became much easier to apply for jobs in various areas of the company.

Each task force must also consider whether its approach to implementation should be either *pragmatic* or *accelerated*, as illustrated in Figure 8.10. Pragmatic implementation is characterized by initially slower rollout to fewer locations, followed by implementation in a greater number of locations at a later time. The advantages to this approach include more time to conduct thorough communications and training, the ability to apply learning from early implementation locations to later locations, and the option to use managers and employees from early implementation sites to communicate and train at later sites. The disadvantages are that some changes will not lend themselves to implementation in only one part of the organization, that locations not implementing early will build resistance to the changes, that later locations may see the changes as unimportant because their implementation can be post-

Figure 8.10 Pragmatic Versus Accelerated Implementation

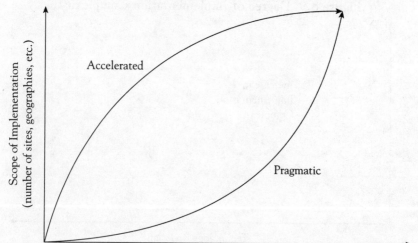

poned, and that the company will be running two parallel systems longer, which may cause confusion both internal and external to the company.

Accelerated implementation is typified by initially faster rollout to a larger number of locations, if not all locations at once. The advantages are that all locations will view the change as important due to the broad initial rollout, that two simultaneous systems will not exist, and that the results from the changes will likely be realized sooner and more broadly. The disadvantages are that the organization does not have "pilots" (sites with earlier implementation) from which to learn.

Reviewing Implementation Plans

Once the ATFs have drafted detailed implementation plans, the task force leaders should meet as the core team to review the implementation plans in aggregate. (This is the two-day core team implementation plans review workshop identified on the road map in Figure 8.11.) The purpose of the two-day session is for the task force leaders to (1) review the implementation plans for completeness, (2) identify overlaps in the implementation plans across the task forces, and (3) prepare for presenting the implementation plans to the advisory team. The workshop helps the task force leaders to assess the cumulative effect of the plans, identify priorities, and pinpoint overlaps and gaps. Appendix B provides a sample outline for the two-day implementation plans review session.

After the core team implementation plans review session, the task forces need to take the feedback received and augment their plans. For example, does the plan have enough detail? Does the time line make sense? Is the plan too complex? Is each task force coordinating with all the other task forces it needs to? Have all of the people who need to assist with implementation (executives, managers, employees, others) been included? The task force needs to address these issues during the week leading up to the advisory team implementation plans review meeting.

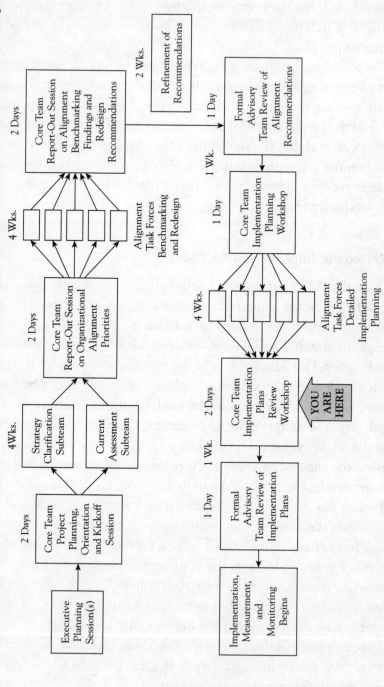

Figure 8.11 Typical Making Strategy Work Project Road Map: Implementation Plans Review Workshop

Approximately sixteen weeks from two-day kickoff session to beginning of implementation.

Formal Advisory Team Implementation Plans Review

After the task forces refine their implementation plans, they present them to the advisory team for a formal review (see Figure 8.12). As at the earlier advisory team recommendations review, there should be no surprises during the meeting. Throughout the task forces' work on their implementation plans, the project manager should have been keeping the members of the advisory team updated as to the progress and direction of the groups and the content being developed.

Depending on the complexity and scale of the plans, this advisory team review session usually lasts from four to six hours (sometimes longer). An agenda should be developed by the project manager and given to all participants before the meeting. The meeting room should be large enough to comfortably contain all attendees. Typically the participants include all members of the advisory team, the project manager, and all members of the core team (who are also the task force leaders). Similar to the earlier meeting with the advisory team, during this meeting the recommendations can be presented either by one person, such as the project manager, or by each task force leader in turn. There should also be a note taker to record the feedback given by the advisory team regarding each task force's implementation plans. See Appendix B for a sample outline of an advisory team implementation plans review session.

Three key outputs should result from this review session:

1. Executive consensus and commitment to implement redesigned, high-priority organizational influence systems that will build competitive advantage for the organization

2. Executive commitment to actively participate in implementation activities

3. Agreed-upon measures to track and adjust the redesigned influence systems

Figure 8.12 Typical Making Strategy Work Project Road Map: Review of Implementation Plans

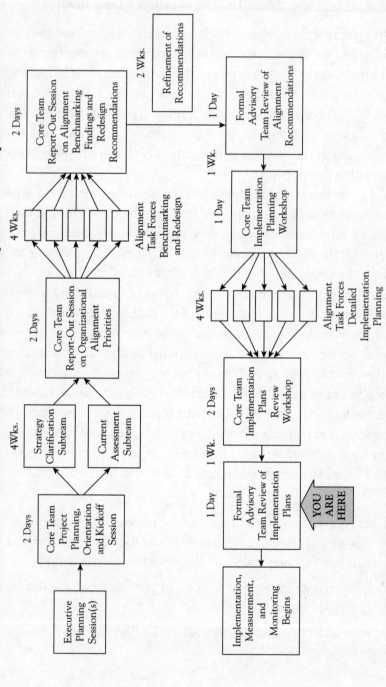

Approximately sixteen weeks from two-day kickoff session to beginning of implementation.

An excellent example of a strategy implementation that was not only well-planned but also well-executed comes from a large department store chain that redesigned several of its influence systems to deploy a customer service growth strategy. The process of implementation began with the most senior levels of management (approximately fifty people) participating in a three-day workshop that detailed the changes that would be occurring to several of the company's influence systems (training, communications, goals and measures, rewards and recognition, the physical environment, and so on). The three-day session also identified the executives' roles during implementation (delivering training, conducting key meetings, and so forth). Within the next two months, executives participated in delivering customer service training to the company's management and employees in more than 1,100 stores across the United States. Additionally, the president of the company personally delivered monthly communications via video to all locations. Immediately following each monthly communication from the president, executives and store management were given briefing notes to use during meetings with their direct reports to discuss and extend the president's message. Moreover, feedback from the follow-up meetings was passed back to the strategy implementation project manager and core team every month, to be acted upon as necessary. Finally, management simplified the measurement system of the company to focus on two key elements: sales and service (by store employees), and people management (by all executives and store managers). Redesigning the company's influence systems and conducting a well-executed process to implement the changes resulted in a gain of more than five percentage points in company sales during the first year of deploying the service strategy.

Conclusion

Redesigning influence systems, gaining advisory team approval for the redesigns, and beginning implementation are crucial elements of the Making Strategy Work process. Detailed designs and implementation plans will help implementation move more smoothly than if the plans are superficial. Details (for example, logistics, equipment, communications, education, and so on) make or break implementation. Moreover, without advisory team commitment to participate in making the changes happen (through making presentations, participating in employee question-and-answer sessions, and so on) the implementation will falter. Once implementation begins, the effort is by no means complete. The next tasks are to measure the impact and refine the process moving forward. These are detailed in the next chapter.

Chapter Nine

Measuring the Impact and Refining the Process

The last thing that most companies need is more measures layered on top of already overwhelming data generation exercises. Information overload is all too common in today's organizations. The explosion of information technology also has caused an eruption of available information. Functions such as finance, marketing, systems, human resources, design, production, logistics, real estate, and so on all produce heaps of data. Ratios, statistics, costs, trends, comparisons, and the like are all fair game. Moreover, the frequency of measurement is not just year to year, it is also month to month, week to week, day to day, and hour to hour. Available information is not the issue. What many companies do not need is more measurement; what they do need is more *focus* in their measurement systems.

Measurement and refinement is the final stage of the Making Strategy Work project (see Figures 9.1 and 9.2). Measures should be identified at two key points in the project. First, the task forces should initially identify potential measures during their benchmarking and redesign work. Task forces often will ask benchmarked companies about how they measure their influence systems. From these companies' responses much can be learned. The methods by which other companies measure often provide valuable and creative ideas. Second, the task forces should include measures in the design of their detailed implementation plans. Then, as the core team integrates the implementation plans, it should also integrate the measures recommended by the task forces. If this is not done, the separate measures developed by each task force will be only

**Figure 9.1 The Six Stages of the
Making Strategy Work Project: Stage Six**

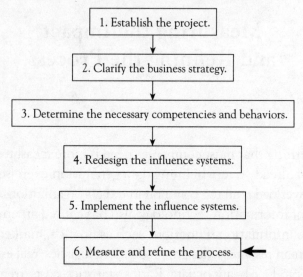

marginally effective, or worse, measures will be duplicated. Coordination of measures by the core team will ensure that these outcomes do not occur.

Value Versus Efficiency

As a result of reengineering, many companies have installed measures to illustrate the efficiency and cost-effectiveness of activities associated with the twelve influence systems. These types of transactional measures include such quantification as the cost of each new hire, the ratio of system employees to total company employees, or the cost of training per employee. However, efficiency measures provide little evidence of the actual value that the influence systems provide to implementing company strategy. This conclusion is supported by People Management Resources (1995) in their publication entitled, *Action Guide: How to Measure the Impact of Your Company's People Practices,* in which they state, "The problem with transaction-based measurement practices is they focus

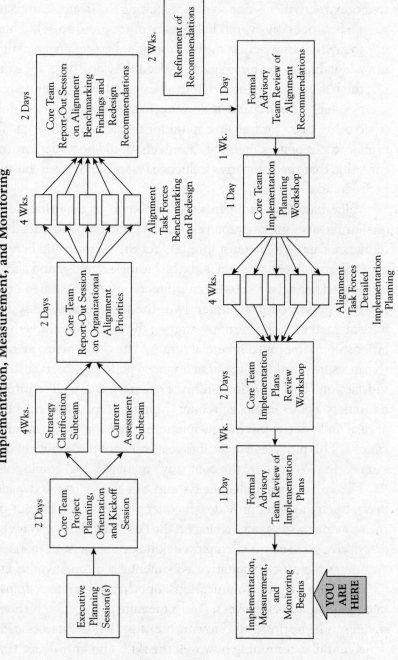

Figure 9.2 Typical Making Strategy Work Project Road Map: Implementation, Measurement, and Monitoring

Executive Planning Session(s)

2 Days — Core Team Project Planning, Orientation and Kickoff Session

4 Wks. — Strategy Clarification Subteam / Current Assessment Subteam

2 Days — Core Team Report-Out Session on Organizational Alignment Priorities

4 Wks. — Alignment Task Forces Benchmarking and Redesign

2 Days — Core Team Report-Out Session on Alignment Benchmarking Findings and Redesign Recommendations

2 Wks. — Refinement of Recommendations

1 Day — Formal Advisory Team Review of Alignment Recommendations

1 Wk. — Core Team Implementation Planning Workshop

1 Day

4 Wks. — Alignment Task Forces Detailed Implementation Planning

2 Days — Core Team Implementation Plans Review Workshop

1 Wk. — Formal Advisory Team Review of Implementation Plans

1 Day — Implementation, Measurement, and Monitoring Begins

YOU ARE HERE

almost entirely on cost avoidance, i.e., measuring the efficiency of traditional activities—not on demonstrating the strategic impact of people practices on overall business performance" (p. 4). That is not to say that transaction measurement and cost management do not add value to an organization. Indeed they do. Take, for example, the business advantages that can be gained from generated cost savings, such as being able to lower prices, make people available to do other tasks, or free up capital for needed investments. The primary focus of measurement, however, should be to demonstrate the value that the company's influence systems provide to business performance.

Value-based measurements can embody both quantitative and qualitative assessment and reporting. *Quantitatively*, financial performance captures the most interest. Yet the relationship between aligning an influence system with the business strategy and achieving desired financial results is not a direct one. As illustrated by the research presented in Chapter Two, the more influence systems were aligned with the business strategy, the more direct was the relationship to improved financial results. The other main quantitative measure of value, aside from financial performance, is customer satisfaction. This measure can involve external as well as internal customers. For example, a premier shipping company conducts an annual audit of the internal recipients of the company's communications. This provides a quantitative measure of the quality of communications as rated by the company's managers and employees.

The value of the influence systems can also be assessed *qualitatively*. Such measures provide a broader picture of the impact that the influence systems are having on the company. They can include descriptive assessments of employee skill development by managers. Another widely used qualitative assessment is written or verbal evaluation of training, communications, or other influence systems by management and employees. And a measure of the effectiveness of staffing and selection is the growing use of *skill alignment* assessments, which entail determining how well the skills and knowledge that a person possesses match the position for which he or she was hired.

A danger of developing both quantitative and qualitative measures is that companies may become overloaded with too many measures. A way of keeping measurement focused while applying multiple sets of quantitative and qualitative measures was introduced by Robert Kaplan and David Norton in their 1992 *Harvard Business Review* article entitled "The Balanced Scorecard: Measures That Drive Performance." In the article, the authors present a means of measuring a company's progress toward its strategic goals that entails four core areas of performance: (1) financial, (2) customers, (3) internal processes, and (4) innovation and improvement activities. This approach provides organizations with a means of assessing not only the value of the influence systems but also the organization's progress toward desired strategic outcomes. Although the "balanced scorecard" presented by Kaplan and Norton may not be the panacea for all organizations, it does provide a robust method for developing a comprehensive, consolidated metric of strategy implementation.

Beyond Employee Satisfaction

A measure that has been widely used in many companies is employee opinion surveys. Using them in their traditional form, however, is not the way to measure the effectiveness of strategy implementation. Typically, employee opinion surveys measure "satisfaction." Measuring whether people are satisfied with their work environment provides little in the way of useful information by which to manage the business. Worse yet, employee satisfaction is not a measure of strategy implementation. What should be assessed is both employees' and management's *commitment* to and *alignment* with the business strategy—not whether people like working for the company. Survey items such as "My manager clearly communicates goals and measures to me," "My manager provides clear and frequent performance feedback to me," "I understand our unit's financial and operating goals," or "My manager and I have agreed on the skills and knowledge that I will work on developing over the next year" are examples of *alignment survey items* rather than satisfaction survey items.

Alignment survey items such as these are used every six months at AT&T's Global Business Communications Systems unit. The survey, known as the Associate Value Index, focuses on assessing the development opportunities that managers provide for their employees. Moreover, management incentive pay is attached to the index ratings, resulting in a 62 percent improvement in "associate value" ratings from 1991 to 1994 (Nellis and Lane, 1995).

Building Accountability

Once measures are developed, they should be used to build accountability among management and employees. Accountability can be achieved through several mechanisms. First, measures should be *made public* through broad communication to the organization. People should be made aware of the measures, how they will be used, the performance they are intended to drive, and so forth. Second, measures should be *routinely tracked*. Whether daily, weekly, monthly, or otherwise, measurement should be done regularly to help set people's expectations. Third, progress should be *regularly reviewed and reported*. For example, progress against measurement criteria can be reviewed at management meetings or conferences, or published in quarterly reports. Fourth, measures should be *linked to performance*. Improvement goals can be incorporated into management and employee performance plans, identifying targets, thresholds, and/or desired trends.

Course Corrections

Too often measurements are just "nice to know." Every effort should be made to ensure that this does not occur. The measurements used should *trigger actions* for needed adjustments to the influence systems once implementation begins. No matter how detailed the planning, how extensive the communications, and how well conducted the education, any implementation effort will be flawed at the beginning. "Going live" must always entail course adjustments along the way. Furthermore, course corrections are often more frequent in the beginning of implementation in order to work out the bugs. Believing that implementation begins and ends on day one is a severe mistake. Regular measurement that spurs corrective action helps to smooth out the flaws as implementation progresses. For this reason, a component of the advisory team, the core team, and the alignment task forces should stay intact for at least a few months after implementation begins. Doing so facilitates the identification, approval, and execution of key adjustments in a timely manner.

Besides improving the influence systems during implementation, measurement should feed into refining the strategic planning process as well as the contents of the business strategy. For example, employee and management feedback should indicate the effectiveness of the input process used. Likewise, customer input solicited along with financial measures should witness to the effectiveness of sales and service activities, the impact of new operating procedures, or the appeal of new products. Using information of this kind will help the company adjust the business strategy itself and the approach taken to develop it.

Conclusion

Neither quantitative nor qualitative measures alone create a comprehensive picture of the value that influence systems contribute to the achievement of a business strategy. It takes both types of assessment to provide the information required to improve the strategy implementation process and adjust the influence systems on an ongoing basis. Moreover, measures not used to build the accountability of management and employees will ultimately fail due to lack of commitment to acting on the information.

The following basic steps for developing effective, focused measures will help ensure that the influence systems are adding value to the achievement of the company's business strategy:

- Have each task force generate a broad list of possible measures for the priority influence system it redesigned.

- Have each task force narrow down its list to no more than two or three key measures (use existing assessment mechanisms and collection tools whenever appropriate) and submit a short list to the core team.
- Have the core team solicit input from management and employees about their reactions to the measurement short list.
- Have the core team refine the short list based on the gathered input.
- Have the core team obtain the advisory team's agreement on the measures.
- Have the task forces and core team establish a baseline of current performance for the agreed-upon measures.
- Have the task forces and core team set preliminary performance targets for each measure.
- Have the core team obtain agreement on the performance targets from the advisory team.
- Have the core team, with the approval of the advisory team, establish accountability mechanisms for the measures, such as incorporating key measures into management and employee performance plans, setting regular measurement reporting processes, and so forth.
- Have the key executives and members of the advisory team communicate the measures to customers and the organization.
- Have the task forces, the core team, and others as identified begin the measurement process when deployment starts, and continue throughout implementation.
- On the basis of the assessment information obtained, have the core team, and others as identified, communicate progress to customers and the organization and make adjustments to the influence systems and/or business strategy as necessary, with the approval of the advisory team.

Chapter Ten

Putting It All Together

By now the reader should be very familiar with the Making Strategy Work project road map, originally introduced in Figure 3.4, which presents a pragmatic process that organizations can apply to accomplish strategy implementation. The Making Strategy Work process (described in Chapters Three through Nine) is meant to serve as a model for companies, business units, and even departments that need to implement their strategies more effectively. On the basis of a company's size, its location, and its history of strategy implementation, the process can (and should) be adapted to the situation. It can be accelerated or decelerated depending on company needs, available resources, and the complexity of strategies and implementation issues. However, the foundations of the Making Strategy Work process should be kept intact. The basis of the process is to take an *integrated approach* to strategy implementation, which entails the following:

- Involving line and functional management and employees
- Applying a project approach
- Assigning responsibilities that ensure that planning and implementation tasks are completed
- Ensuring clear and planned communication throughout the process
- Actively involving executives (such as in delivering messages, conducting training, and so on)
- Regularly measuring progress against desired goals

- Making the strategy planning and implementation process part of the daily running of the business rather than a side issue

Can We Start in the Middle?

Yes, many Making Strategy Work processes do start in the middle. For example, companies often begin by looking to benchmarking information for ideas on creating strategic change, or they have a desire to put a new compensation and rewards system in place to support a strategic push. However, in the scheme of making strategy work that is presented in this book, these and other midstream activities dictate that a company must look upstream before going downstream to complete the activity they started.

For instance, to put a new compensation and rewards system in place, companies must first understand *what* the system should reinforce in the context of the business strategy. Consequently, firms need to understand their business strategy, and the competencies they need to create and reinforce through a new reward system. To obtain these understandings, firms must undertake the early steps of the Making Strategy Work process—clarifying the business strategy and determining the competencies and behaviors that will support that strategy. Once they have achieved these understandings, companies can more effectively redesign a reward system, for example.

It Won't Happen Overnight

The tendency of companies that do not experience an immediate shift in financial performance when attempting to implement their strategies is to change direction. They almost automatically try another reward system, cut back or reorient training, change the organization structure again, and so on. "Flavor of the month" becomes the rallying cry from employees and management alike. The fact of the matter is that strategy implementation does not occur overnight. Instituting organizational behavior changes and developing competencies are vastly more challenging and time-consuming than either making financial changes (such as buying or selling a business unit, downsizing, and so on) or making operational changes (such as automating a process, changing the steps in a process, and so forth)(see Figure 10.1). This is why so many organizations prefer to take easy routes to short-term profitability rather than pursue strategies of long-term growth. However, companies inevitably will need to contend with the fact that there are only limited channels available to create short-term spikes in earnings. To create and sustain long-term growth and profitability, firms must take on the many challenges of creating organizational behavior changes and developing core competencies.

Bigger Is Not Better

Making strategy work by focusing resources, realigning the influence systems, and maintaining a strategic purpose for implementation actions does not necessitate building up huge administrative support functions such as information systems or human resources. Unfortunately, the knee-jerk reaction of management when looking

**Figure 10.1 The Relative Ease of
Behavior Change and Competency Development**

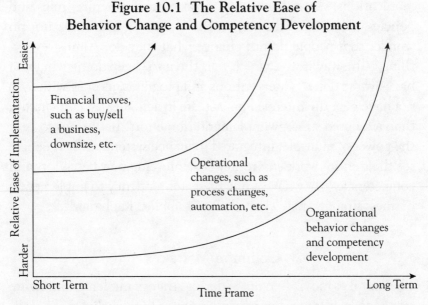

Note: Special thanks to Kevin Sullivan of Wells Fargo for his insights and input into this diagram.

at undertaking a concerted strategy implementation effort is to be scared by the seemingly large investment of capital, time, and other resources. However, by coordinating a strategy implementation effort vis-à-vis a project approach like the one presented in this book, companies can control the investment they make, prioritize how their investment is utilized, assess the return on the investment they make, and measure progress against their desired strategic goals.

It is ironic that under the banner of cost-effectiveness, organizations approach strategy implementation from a piecemeal perspective, employing a new program here or undertaking an "intervention" there. Doing so only throws good money after bad. Management is constantly confounded by the lack of impact that a redesigned compensation program has, or by the little difference that new training has made. Yet there should be no mystery to the lack of effectiveness of these efforts. For example, when management and employees are told about a new rewards program that is meant to create the behavior and competencies that reinforce the strategy of the company, but the rest of the influence systems (such as training, communications, senior leadership, organization structure, rules and policies, and so on) still support the old way of operating, it is no wonder that people do not change what they do. Almost everything is the way it was, which tells them to "keep doing what you have always done." Interventions and programs, most of which do not have near the intended impact, are in actuality *less cost-effective* than a focused strategy implementation effort that brings to bear the power of multiple, integrated influence systems. When people see their entire work environment reinforcing new behaviors and competencies, they have a much greater tendency to implement a business strategy than when change is applied haphazardly.

Common Mistakes

The mistakes most often made during strategy implementation are related to lack of focus and coordination, and the belief that a well-designed strategy will implement itself. The following errors are the *seven deadly sins of strategy implementation:*

1. Lack of leadership
2. A focus on only one or two influence systems (an *intervention* approach)
3. Unclear or inadequate project management
4. Poor communication throughout the process
5. Applying insufficient resources to the effort
6. Easing into and through the changes to the influence systems
7. Waiting until the strategy is completely developed before starting implementation activities

The first sin, *lack of leadership*, results when senior management attempts to delegate strategy implementation. And worse, when they do attempt to devote time to the necessary actions, they grossly underestimate the actual time needed. Conducting key communication events, delivering portions of training sessions, participating on the advisory team, and so forth all take time. Moreover, they are activities that must be priorities. When people see leadership postponing events related to strategy implementation, they too postpone their actions to implement the strategy.

Sins two through five all have to do with not employing a coordinated project approach to strategy implementation. Poor project management, undercommunication, inadequate project resources, and taking a programmatic approach to redesigning the influence systems will all derail even the best-planned strategies. Moreover, even after a well-coordinated redesign of the influence systems has been conducted, the sixth sin is to ease into and through the recommended changes to the influence systems. Taking too long during implementation only creates anxiety among management and employees. Changing rewards, training, communications, organization structure, rules and policies, and so on raises questions in people's minds, such as How will my pay be effected? Will I have a job? Will I have to move? or Will I be able to learn the right skills for the future? Moving slowly during implementation only prolongs answering these questions, and gives people excuses to focus on themselves rather than on what needs to be done to implement the strategy effectively.

Finally, the seventh sin is to wait until the strategy is completely developed before starting implementation activities. During strategy formulation, the structure of the Making Strategy Work project can be established and communications efforts can be initiated. Also, the changes that might be required to each influence system should be anticipated on the basis of the strategies being deliberated. Doing so often helps management to determine which strategies to pursue. When managers believe that they are not willing or able to do what it will take to implement a strategy being considered, they should probably take the strategy off their list of possibilities because it will ultimately fail anyway.

Key Success Factors

When management and employees from both line and support functions are asked what the key factors are in creating a successful strategy implementation effort, their responses converge. Their collective comments form the following ten key success factors for making strategy work:

- Senior management support and commitment
- Linkage with the overall business strategy
- Identified competencies that support the business strategy
- Compelling business reason for change
- Clearly defined approach
- Highly respected and capable project leader
- Use of best practices
- Involvement of line and support function management and employees
- Measurable goals and objectives
- Ongoing communication and feedback between the project team and key constituents of the organization

Conclusion

Many companies have become expert at making strategy, but unfortunately few have become good at making their strategy work. There should be no illusions. Making strategy work is not easy. It takes *focus*. It takes *resources*. It takes *commitment*. It takes *time*. And it takes *effort*. These are assets that many firms have spread very thin as of late. If management is serious about a growth strategy, they need to get serious about implementation. The way they demonstrate their conviction is through the effort and resources they put into strategy implementation. The bottom line is that companies *must realign and integrate* their organizational influence systems to support their growth plans or even the best-planned strategies *will not* work.

Advisory Team Guidebook

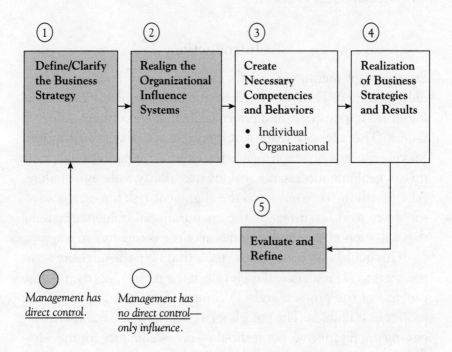

| ① Define/Clarify the Business Strategy | ② Realign the Organizational Influence Systems | ③ Create Necessary Competencies and Behaviors | ④ Realization of Business Strategies and Results |

③ Create Necessary Competencies and Behaviors
- Individual
- Organizational

⑤ Evaluate and Refine

● *Management has <u>direct control</u>.*

○ *Management has <u>no direct control</u>— only influence.*

Contents

I. Introduction

Strategy implementation calls for clear goals, coordination, and detailed planning. The way in which strategy implementation is communicated, sponsored, and prioritized will mean either success or failure. The advisory team is responsible for that prioritization. Making the strategy implementation effort an organizational priority will facilitate success; not making it a priority will ensure failure. Along with the core team and the alignment task forces, the advisory team works to integrate the organizational influence systems that will support the implementation of the company's strategy.

This guidebook contains the tools that help the advisory team members to (1) understand their role in the project, (2) oversee the progress of the project, and (3) communicate the impact of the project as it unfolds. The guidebook is not meant to be all-encompassing or prescriptive, but it should serve as guidance for the advisory team. Using it will help the advisory team to coordinate its Making Strategy Work efforts so that the process is focused, practical, and successful.

II. Making Strategy Work Project Road Map

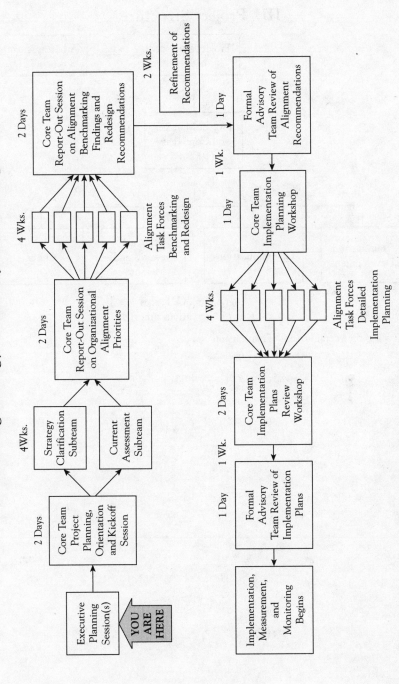

Approximately sixteen weeks from two-day kickoff session to beginning of implementation.

III. Project Structure

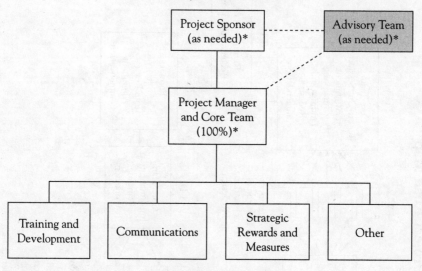

Alignment Task Forces
(up to 75% at various times)*

*Typical time commitment of participants

IV. Project Roles

Project Constituent	Roles	Sample Tasks
Advisory team	• Are vocal, visible leaders of the strategy deployment effort • Provide oversight, direction, and review • Participate in the delivery of key messages	• Present strategy implementation messages in key meetings throughout company • Assist the project sponsor in selecting the project manager and core team members • Meet with the core team for regular progress reviews
Project sponsor	• Has day-to-day oversight of project progress • Assists core team with key decisions (for example, task force overlaps that cannot be resolved by the core team)	• Present key messages in meetings with the advisory team • Communicate with managers to free up resources to staff the project
Project manager	• Oversees project planning and coordination • Communicates project progress • Manages the core team	• Develop project Gantt chart • Conduct core team meetings • Provide regular progress updates to the project sponsor
Core team	• Oversee project coordination • Oversee project communication • Lead alignment task forces	• Oversee selection, staffing, and kickoff of task forces • Hold regular meetings to review progress reports and measures • Present progress and recommendations to the advisory team and other organizational entities as scheduled
Alignment task forces	• Work on subprojects to align particular influence systems with the business strategy • Participate in project communication	• Prepare a plan for changes to their particular influence system • Present recommendations to the core team and advisory team • Coordinate and communicate with other task forces as needed to address overlaps and gaps

V. Advisory Team Areas of Focus

Project Oversight and Direction

Oversight of the project entails giving feedback and direction to the core team and task forces to assist them with their work.

Project Communications

Members of the advisory team will often be called upon to deliver key messages about the project and its impact on the organization. This will help to facilitate the success of the project by ensuring that all stakeholders are kept informed of project goals, progress, and outcomes.

Identification and Clarification of the Business Strategy and Necessary Competencies

The advisory team is made up of people in the organization who have a lot of input into identifying the key elements of the business strategy and the competencies needed to support the strategy. They should provide their insights and direction on company strategy to the core team as needed.

Review of Recommendations for Realigning and Implementing Redesigned Influence Systems

The advisory team will be called upon to review the implementation plans developed by the core team and task forces. Team members should be prepared to provide the core team and task forces with feedback, adjustments, and approval for go-ahead as appropriate.

VI. Project Communications

A primary responsibility of the advisory team is to ensure that a well-planned strategy for project communication is implemented. The project manager usually takes primary responsibility for developing the following communications matrix.

Stakeholders (Who?)	Objective (Why?)	Message (What?)	Vehicle (How?)	How Often (When?)	Responsibility (Who Delivers?)
Executive Management	Explanation of overall strategy implementation effort	Reasons for a dedicated strategy implementation effort Project structure, goals, objectives, and time line	Meeting	10/01	CEO
All Management and Employees	Explanation of overall strategy implementation effort	Project structure, goals, objectives, and time line	Newsletter E-mail Department meetings	U.S. 10/03 Europe 10/4	Executives

Source: Adapted from Galpin, 1996.

VII. Measurement Guidelines

The following steps will help to ensure the development of focused, effective measures that should be used throughout implementation:

- Have each task force generate a broad list of possible measures for the priority influence system it redesigned.

- Have each task force narrow down its list to no more than two or three key measures (use existing assessment mechanisms and collection tools whenever appropriate) and submit a short list to the core team.

- Have the core team solicit input from management and employees about their reactions to the measurement short list.

- Have the core team refine the short list based on the gathered input.

- Have the core team obtain the advisory team's agreement on the measures.

- Have the task forces and core team establish a baseline of current performance for the agreed-upon measures.

- Have the task forces and core team set preliminary performance targets for each measure.

- Have the core team obtain agreement on the performance targets from the advisory team.

- Have the core team, with the approval of the advisory team, establish accountability mechanisms for the measures, such as incorporating key measures into management and employee performance plans, setting regular measurement reporting processes, and so forth.

- Have the key executives and members of the advisory team communicate the measures to customers and the organization.

- Have the task forces, the core team, and others as identified begin the measurement process when deployment starts, and continue throughout implementation.

- On the basis of the assessment information obtained, have the core team, and others as identified, communicate progress to customers and the organization and make adjustments to the influence systems and/or business strategy as necessary, with the approval of the advisory team.

Appendix B

Core Team Guidebook

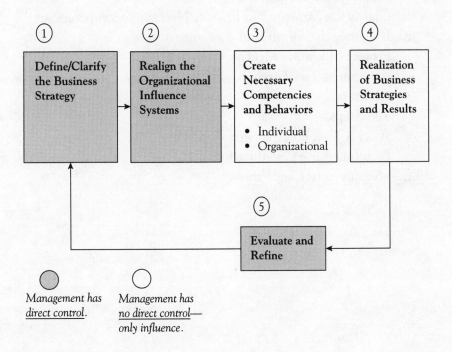

(1) **Define/Clarify the Business Strategy**

(2) **Realign the Organizational Influence Systems**

(3) **Create Necessary Competencies and Behaviors**
- Individual
- Organizational

(4) **Realization of Business Strategies and Results**

(5) **Evaluate and Refine**

Management has direct control.

Management has no direct control—only influence.

Contents

I. Introduction

Strategy implementation calls for clear goals, coordination, and detailed planning. The way in which strategy implementation is coordinated sets the stage for an integrated effort. The core team is responsible for that coordination. Together with the alignment task forces and the advisory teams, the core team works to integrate the organizational influence systems that will facilitate the success of the company's strategy.

This guidebook contains the tools that help the core team to (1) understand their role in the project, (2) clarify the business strategy and necessary competencies, (3) coordinate the work of the task forces, and (4) report on progress to the advisory team. The guidebook is not meant to be all-encompassing or prescriptive, but it should serve as a starting point for the core team. Using it will help the core team to coordinate its Making Strategy Work efforts so that the process is focused, practical, and successful.

II. Project Road Map

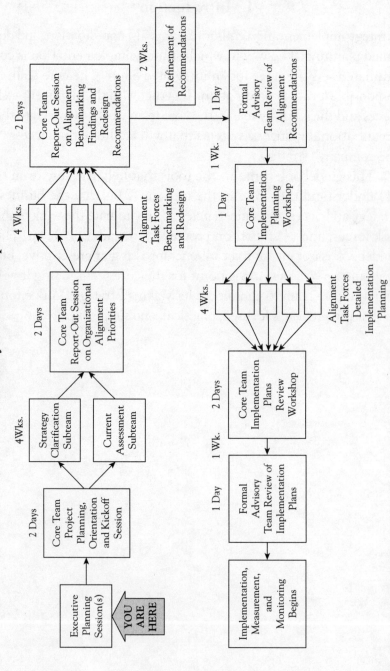

Approximately sixteen weeks from two-day kickoff session to beginning of implementation.

III. Project Structure

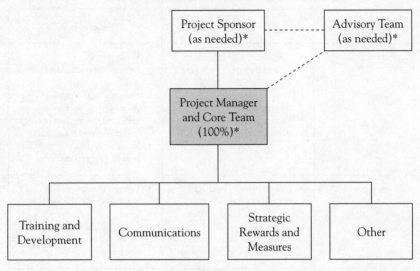

Alignment Task Forces
(up to 75% at various times)*

*Typical time commitment of participants.

IV. Project Roles

Project Constituent	Roles	Sample Tasks
Advisory team	• Are vocal, visible leaders of the strategy deployment effort • Provide oversight, direction, and review • Participate in the delivery of key messages	• Present strategy implementation messages in key meetings throughout company • Assist the project sponsor in selecting the project manager and core team members • Meet with the core team for regular progress reviews
Project sponsor	• Has day-to-day oversight of project progress • Assists core team with key decisions (for example, task force overlaps that cannot be resolved by the core team)	• Present key messages in meetings with the advisory team • Communicate with managers to free up resources to staff the project
Project manager	• Oversees project planning and coordination • Communicates project progress • Manages the core team	• Develop project Gantt chart • Conduct core team meetings • Provide regular progress updates to the project sponsor
Core team	• Oversee project coordination • Oversee project communication • Lead alignment task forces	• Oversee selection, staffing, and kickoff of task forces • Hold regular meetings to review progress reports and measures • Present progress and recommendations to the advisory team and other organizational entities as scheduled
Alignment task forces	• Work on subprojects to align particular influence systems with the business strategy • Participate in project communication	• Prepare a plan for changes to their particular influence system • Present recommendations to the core team and advisory team • Coordinate and communicate with other task forces as needed to address overlaps and gaps

V. Core Team Areas of Focus

Overall Project Management

The core team is responsible for coordination (that is, project management) of the alignment task forces, review and approval of the implementation plans developed by the task forces, and project tracking and measurement.

Project Communications

The core team develops the communications strategy and the messages that must be sent out on a regular basis to keep stakeholders informed.

Clarify the Business Strategy

The core team interviews key executives and others to identify and clarify the key elements of the business strategy and the competencies necessary to support the strategy.

Assess the Current Influence Systems

The core team conducts an initial assessment of the company's current practices in the influence systems. The results of the assessment will be used to prioritize those systems that will be redesigned by the alignment task forces.

VI. Core Team Logistics

Leadership

The project manager is the leader of the core team. This person will act as contact for the core team and/or advisory team and will have primary responsibility for coordinating the overall activities of the core team.

Communications

The core team should set up a communication protocol and decide on tools to be used in exchanging information among the core team members and with the task forces. This protocol may include setting up e-mail addresses, constructing distribution lists, agreeing on meeting places, and so on.

Meetings

The core team should meet as often and for as long as necessary—as often as two or three times a week initially, or as infrequently as once every week. It is also important that someone be assigned to record meeting notes that identify key actions that need to be completed, as well as future meeting dates and times. Additionally, formal work sessions are scheduled for the core team alone and with the advisory team, at key milestones throughout the project (see the project road map in section II of this guidebook).

VII. Project Communications

A key responsibility of the project manager and core team is to ensure that a well-planned project communication strategy is implemented. Such a strategy will help to facilitate the success of the project by ensuring that all stakeholders are kept informed of project goals and progress. The following communication matrix is a useful tool for planning the project's communication strategy. The matrix should be revised during each major stage of the project (such as at kickoff, implementation planning, and review).

Stakeholders (Who?)	Objective (Why?)	Message (What?)	Vehicle (How?)	How Often (When?)	Responsibility (Who Delivers?)
Executive Management	Explanation of overall strategy implementation effort	Reasons for a dedicated strategy implementation effort Project structure, goals, objectives, and time line	Meeting	10/01	CEO
All Management and Employees	Explanation of overall strategy implementation effort	Project structure, goals, objectives, and time line	Newsletter E-mail Department meetings	U.S. 10/03 Europe 10/4	Executives

Source: Adapted from Galpin, 1996.

VIII. Clarify the Strategy and Identify Necessary Competencies

The following matrix can be used by the strategy clarification sub-team during its clarification of the company's strategy and business intentions.

Business Unit	Core Elements of Strategy (shrink, grow, harvest, establish a new business, acquire, add new products, etc.)	Desired Outcomes/ Business Goals and Time Frames (establish a new market, grow revenue, enhance profitability, increase market share, etc.)	Responsibility/ Ownership
Corporate-wide			
Unit A			
Unit B			
Unit C			
Unit D			

The following questions can also be used by the strategy clarification subteam to help clarify the company's strategy and to determine the necessary competencies and behaviors that will support the strategy:

- What will be the driving force or forces of company success over the next five years?

    Customer satisfaction

    Financial stability

    Human resources/employees

    New products/services

Quality improvement
Technological innovations
Operational efficiency
Speed to market
Marketing, advertising, and sales

- What behaviors and competencies will be needed to achieve the business strategy?

Technical skills
Problem-solving skills
Interpersonal skills
Independent judgment and initiative
Leadership skills
Project management skills
Communication skills
General business skills
Financial skills
Customer service and sales skills
Teamwork skills
Others

IX. Influence Systems Initial Assessment

The following survey can be used by the core team during the initial assessment of the current practices of the company's influence systems.

Influence System	Current Effectiveness*			Future Importance in Achieving/ Supporting the Business Plan*			Comments/ Suggestions for Improvement
Goals and Measures	High	Med.	Low	High	Med.	Low	
Rewards and Recognition	High	Med.	Low	High	Med.	Low	
Communications	High	Med.	Low	High	Med.	Low	
Training and Development	High	Med.	Low	High	Med.	Low	
Organizational Structure	High	Med.	Low	High	Med.	Low	
Rules and Policies	High	Med.	Low	High	Med.	Low	
Physical Environment	High	Med.	Low	High	Med.	Low	
Information Systems and Knowledge Sharing	High	Med.	Low	High	Med.	Low	
Operational/Process Changes	High	Med.	Low	High	Med.	Low	
Senior Leadership	High	Med.	Low	High	Med.	Low	
Ceremonies and Events	High	Med.	Low	High	Med.	Low	
Staffing, Selection, and Succession	High	Med.	Low	High	Med.	Low	

*Please circle your response for each influence system.

The following summary matrix can be used by the core team to present the results of the initial assessment of the current practices of the company's influence systems.

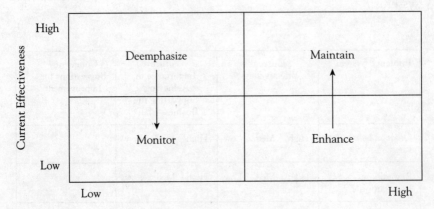

X. Project Milestone Meetings

Throughout the course of the project, the core team will conduct meetings among themselves and with the advisory team at key milestones (see the project road map in section II of this guidebook). The following sample outlines can assist the core team in planning these sessions.

Sample Outline of Core Team Kickoff Meeting Topics

Meeting Objectives
1. Communicate the project purpose, goals, and objectives.
2. Communicate the project time line and key milestones.
3. Identify initial subteams and cross-team communication mechanisms.

Day One
1. Introductions
2. Making strategy work
   The model and the logic
3. Project purpose, goals, and objectives
4. Project constituents
   Advisory team
   Sponsor
   Project manager
   Core team
   Alignment task forces (to be determined by the core team)
5. Initial project subteams
   Strategy clarification and competencies subteam members and leader (subteam one)
   Influence systems assessment subteam members and leader (subteam two)
   Subteams goals and objectives, and due date for core team report-out session
6. Initial strategy deployment communication plan

Day Two
1. Subteam planning session
   Four-week work schedule
   Information needs and sources
   Cross-team communications responsibilities
   Subteam meeting frequency
   Administrative support needs and access

Sample Meeting Topics Outline for
Core Team Report-Out of Organizational Alignment Priorities

Meeting Objectives
- Communicate the core elements of the business strategy.
- Communicate the core competencies and behaviors needed.
- Communicate the influence systems current assessment results.
- Identify influence systems alignment priorities.
- Identify alignment task force leaders.
- Establish cross–task force communication mechanisms.

Day One
1. Introduction and meeting objectives
2. Strategy clarification subteam report-out of
   Core elements of the business strategy
   Core competencies and behaviors needed
3. Influence systems assessment subteam report-out on
   Results of assessment feedback
4. Core team identification of alignment priorities
   Priority influence systems to be realigned with the business strategy
5. Establish alignment task forces and select task force leaders
   One task force per priority influence system
   Task force goals, objectives, and due dates for next report-out session
   One leader per task force chosen from the core team membership
   Leaders to identify other task force members from the organization at large

Day Two
1. Subteam planning session
   Four-week work schedule
   Information needs and sources
   Cross–task force communication responsibilities
   Task force meeting frequency
   Administrative support needs and access
2. Benchmarking
   Who, how, what
   Initial benchmarking plan
3. Redesign
   Need for integration with other task forces
4. Revised project communication plan for this stage of the project

Sample Meeting Topics Outline for Core Team
Benchmarking Findings and Redesign Recommendations

Meeting Objectives

- Communicate each task force's benchmarking findings and recommendations to the other task force leaders.
- Identify overall priorities, gaps, and overlaps among task force recommendations.
- Identify key enablers for implementation that cut across task forces.

Day One

1. Introduction and meeting objectives
2. Task forces report-out on

   Benchmarking findings summary

   Core elements of their recommendations

   Estimated costs and benefits

   Key enablers needed

   Overlaps and integration needed with other task forces

Day Two

1. Determine recommendation priorities
2. Identify refinements needed to be made by each task force

   More clarity or detail

   Less complexity

   Other
3. Identify key enablers across task forces

Sample Meeting Outline for
Advisory Team Recommendations Review Session

Meeting Objectives

- Communicate task force recommendations to the advisory team.
- Solicit feedback from advisory team regarding recommendations.
- Gain advisory team approval to move to detailed implementation planning.

Session Agenda

1. Introduction and meeting objectives
2. Task forces report-out on
   Core elements of their recommendations
   Estimated costs and benefits
   Key enablers needed
   Overlaps and integration with other task forces
3. Task Force: Rewards and Recognition
4. Task Force: Training and Development
5. Task Force: Communications
6. Others
7. Next step:
   Detailed implementation planning—Go/No Go?

Sample Meeting Outline for
Core Team Implementation Planning Workshop

Workshop Objectives

- Clarify feedback from advisory team review session.
- Establish implementation priorities.
- Clarify time line and deliverables due from each task force.

Workshop Agenda

1. Introduction and session objectives
2. Summary of advisory team feedback
   Feedback for each task force
   Overall feedback
3. Implementation priorities
   Identify
   Establish
4. Task Force deliverables
   Detailed implementation plans
   Deliverables due at next core team meeting
5. Updated communication strategy
   Content
   Delivery requirements

Sample Meeting Topics Outline for
Core Team Implementation Plans Review

Meeting Objectives

- Communicate each task force's detailed implementation plans to all task force leaders.
- Identify overall priorities, gaps, and overlaps among task force plans.
- Prepare for the advisory team review meeting.

Day One

1. Introduction and meeting objectives
2. Task forces report-out on

   Core elements of their implementation plans

   Overlaps and integration needed with other task forces during implementation

Day Two

1. Determine implementation priorities
2. Identify refinements each task force needs to make

   More clarity or detail

   Less complexity

   Other
3. Determine advisory team review meeting priorities and format

   Key points to be made to the advisory team

   Actions needed by advisory team members (such as deliver key messages to the organization, participate in training, and so on)

Sample Outline for Advisory Team
Implementation Plans Workshop

Meeting Objectives

- Communicate task force implementation plans to the advisory team.
- Solicit feedback from advisory team regarding the plans.
- Gain advisory team approval to conduct implementation activities.
- Gain advisory team members' commitment to participate in implementation activities (such as deliver key messages, participate in training, and so on).
- Agree with advisory team on the tracking and adjusting mechanisms for the redesigned influence systems.

Session Agenda

1. Introduction and meeting objectives
2. Task forces report-out on
   Core elements of their implementation plans
3. Task Force: Rewards and Recognition
4. Task Force: Training and Development
5. Task Force: Communications
6. Others
7. Recommended tracking and adjusting mechanisms for the redesigned influence systems
8. Actions needed from advisory team during implementation:
   Deliver key messages to the organization
   Participate in training
   Deliver training sessions
   Others
9. Next step
   Conduct implementation activities—Go/No Go?

XI. Alignment Task Forces

Charters

Each alignment task force should receive a working charter from the core team, to provide direction on goals, deliverables, and time lines. The following template is a useful format for task force charters.

Task Force Name: _____

Members: _____ *Leader(s)

_____

_____

_____

_____

_____

Task Force Goals/Deliverables (including due dates):

Reporting/Communication (accountability to whom and how often):

Resource(s) (needs and availability):

Links to Other Task Forces (for cross–task force integration):

Ten Steps

The following ten steps will help guide the task forces through their redesign of the influence systems.

Step	Action / Output	Question
Step One	A: Detail current practices O: Basic understanding of the current influence system	Where are we?
Step Two	A: Conduct benchmarking and best practices O: Comparison with other companies	How do we compare?
Step Three	A: Develop redesign recommendations O: Initial realignment designs	Where are we going?
Step Four	A: Integrate various task force recommendations O: Integrated recommendations	Are we coordinated?
Step Five	A: Gain redesign approval O: Advisory team approval of redesign recommendations	Are we in agreement?
Step Six	A: Develop detailed implementation plans O: Announcements, training materials, logistics, scheduling, and so forth	Are we ready?
Step Seven	A: Gain implementation approval O: Advisory team go-ahead approval	Can we implement?
Step Eight	A: Implement O: Conduct training, make announcements, and so forth	Go
Step Nine	A: Measure, monitor, and adjust O: Process reports, process adjustments	Course corrections
Step Ten	A: Completion O: Disband task forces and celebration	Finish

LEGEND: A = Action
O = Output

Weekly Task Force Progress Updates

A key role of the core team is to manage and coordinate the work of the alignment task forces. The following template can be used by each task force leader to report on progress and next steps. The summary sheet should be delivered to the project manager at the end of each week.

(Used by each task force to update the project manager
at the end of every week about the team's progress.)

Task force name:

Week ending:

1. Key actions during the past week:

2. Key successes:

3a. Key issues:

3b. Potential solutions/help needed:

4. Next steps/actions:

5. Other key information:

Benchmarking Coordination

The following matrix can be used by the project manager and core team to coordinate the benchmarking interviews scheduled by the task forces.

Benchmarked Company	Benchmarked Company Contact Person	Task Forces Wanting to Contact	Date for Scheduled Interview
Company X	• Bob J. • Mary R. • Bob J.	• Training • Rewards • Communications	• 11/10 • 11/11 • 11/10
Company Y	• James S. • Pete W. • Peter M.	• Training • Organizational structure • Knowledge sharing	• 11/12 • 11/13 • 11/14
Company Z	• Susan P. • Pam G. • Bill H.	• Training • Communications • Knowledge sharing	• 11/11 • 11/17 • 11/13

XII. Measurement Guidelines

The following steps will help ensure the development of focused effective measures that should be used throughout implementation.

- Have each task force generate a broad list of possible measures for the priority influence system it redesigned.
- Have each task force narrow down its list to no more than two or three key measures (use existing assessment mechanisms and collection tools whenever appropriate) and submit a short list to the core team.
- Have the core team solicit input from management and employees about their reactions to the measurement short list.
- Have the core team refine the short list based on the gathered input.
- Have the core team obtain the advisory team's agreement on the measures.
- Have the task forces and core team establish a baseline of current performance for the agreed-upon measures.
- Have the task forces and core team set preliminary performance targets for each measure.
- Have the core team obtain agreement on the performance targets from the advisory team.
- Have the core team, with the approval of the advisory team, establish accountability mechanisms for the measures, such as incorporating key measures into management and employee performance plans, setting regular measurement reporting processes, and so forth.
- Have the key executives and members of the advisory team communicate the measures to customers and the organization.
- Have the task forces, the core team, and others as identified begin the measurement process when deployment starts, and continue throughout implementation.

- On the basis of the assessment information obtained, have the core team, and others as identified, communicate progress to customers and the organization and make adjustments to the influence systems and/or business strategy as necessary, with the approval of the advisory team.

Appendix C

Alignment Task Forces Guidebook

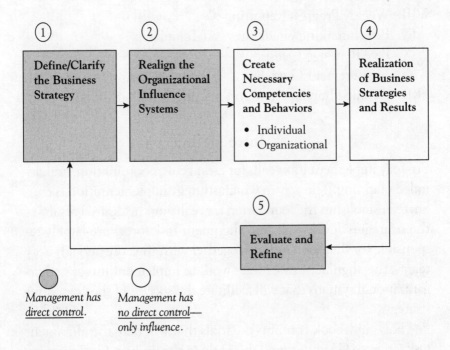

① Define/Clarify the Business Strategy

② Realign the Organizational Influence Systems

③ Create Necessary Competencies and Behaviors
- Individual
- Organizational

④ Realization of Business Strategies and Results

⑤ Evaluate and Refine

○ *Management has <u>direct control</u>.*

○ *Management has <u>no direct control</u>— only influence.*

Contents

I. Introduction

Strategy implementation calls for clear goals, coordination, and detailed planning. The way in which strategy implementation is conducted establishes the foundation for realizing the desired results of the strategies developed. The alignment task forces are largely responsible for that foundation. Together with the core and advisory teams, the alignment task forces work to implement integrated organizational systems that will facilitate the success of the company's strategy.

This guidebook contains the tools that will help the alignment task forces to (1) understand their role in the project, (2) determine their deliverables, (3) develop realignment plans for their influence systems, and (4) implement their plans. The guidebook is not meant to be all-encompassing or prescriptive, but it should serve as a common starting point for every alignment task force. Using it will help the task forces to coordinate their Making Strategy Work efforts so that the process is focused, practical, and successful.

II. Project Road Map

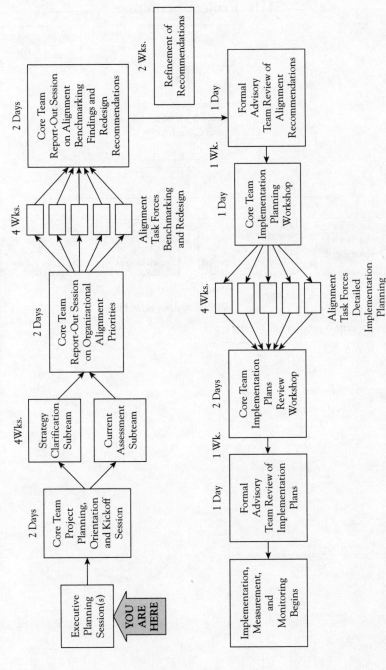

Approximately sixteen weeks from two-day kickoff session to beginning of implementation.

III. Project Structure

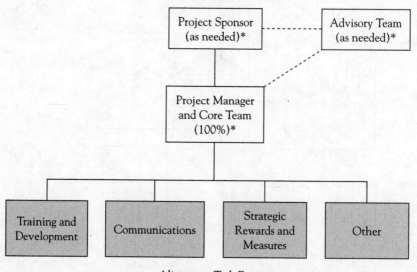

Alignment Task Forces
(up to 75% at various times)*

*Typical time commitment of participants.

IV. Project Roles

Project Constituent	Roles	Sample Tasks
Advisory team	• Are vocal, visible leaders of the strategy deployment effort • Provide oversight, direction, and review • Participate in the delivery of key messages	• Present strategy implementation messages in key meetings throughout company • Assist the project sponsor in selecting the project manager and core team members • Meet with the core team for regular progress reviews
Project sponsor	• Has day-to-day oversight of project progress • Assists core team with key decisions (for example, task force overlaps that cannot be resolved by the core team)	• Present key messages in meetings with the advisory team • Communicate with managers to free up resources to staff the project
Project manager	• Oversees project planning and coordination • Communicates project progress • Manages the core team	• Develop project Gantt chart • Conduct core team meetings • Provide regular progress updates to the project sponsor
Core team	• Oversee project coordination • Oversee project communication • Lead alignment task forces	• Oversee selection, staffing, and kickoff of task forces • Hold regular meetings to review progress reports and measures • Present progress and recommendations to the advisory team and other organizational entities as scheduled
Alignment task forces	• Work on subprojects to align particular influence systems with the business strategy • Participate in communication	• Prepare a plan for changes to their particular influence system • Present recommendations to the core team and advisory team • Coordinate and communicate with other task forces as needed to address overlaps and gaps

V. Task Force Logistics

Leadership

The task force leader is a member of the core team. This person will act as the contact for the core team and/or the advisory team and will have primary responsibility for coordinating the overall activities of the task force.

Project Communications

The task force should set up a communication protocol and decide on tools to be used in exchanging information among members and with other teams. This may include setting up e-mail addresses, constructing distribution lists, agreeing on meeting places, and so on.

Meetings

Task forces should meet as often and for as long as necessary—as often as two or three times a week initially or as infrequently as once every week. It is also important that someone be assigned to record meeting notes that identify key actions that need to be completed, as well as future meeting dates and times.

Weekly Progress Reports

Regardless of whether or not a task force meets weekly, a weekly progress update should be submitted to the project manager. A sample summary progress sheet is included later in this section of the guidebook. Additionally, every week the task force leader will participate in a meeting of the core team to update the other task force leaders on progress and integration needs.

Linkages to Other Task Forces

Many of the task forces will have some overlap or will need to coordinate with one or more other task forces. The team members will need to decide which other task forces they overlap with and how they will link to and communicate with them.

VI. Charter Template

Each alignment task force should receive a working charter from the core team, to provide direction on goals, deliverables, and time lines. The following template is a useful format for task force charters.

Task Force Name: _____

Members: _____ *Leader(s)

                              _____

                              _____

                              _____

                              _____

Task Force Goals/Deliverables (including due dates):

Reporting/Communication (accountability to whom and how often):

Resource(s) (needs and availability):

Links to Other Task Forces (for cross–task force integration):

VII. Ten Steps

The following ten steps will help guide the task forces through their redesign of the influence systems.

Step One	A: Detail current practices O: Basic understanding of the current influence system	Where are we?
Step Two	A: Conduct benchmarking and best practices O: Comparison with other companies	How do we compare?
Step Three	A: Develop redesign recommendations O: Initial realignment designs	Where are we going?
Step Four	A: Integrate various task force recommendations O: Integrated recommendations	Are we coordinated?
Step Five	A: Gain redesign approval O: Advisory team approval of redesign recommendations	Are we in agreement?
Step Six	A: Develop detailed implementation plans O: Announcements, training materials, logistics, scheduling, and so forth	Are we ready?
Step Seven	A: Gain implementation approval O: Advisory team go-ahead approval	Can we implement?
Step Eight	A: Implement O: Conduct training, make announcements, and so forth	Go
Step Nine	A: Measure, monitor, and adjust O: Process reports, process adjustments	Course corrections
Step Ten	A: Completion O: Disband task forces and celebration	Finish

LEGEND: A = Action
         O = Output

VIII. Weekly Progress Reporting

A key role of the core team is to manage and coordinate the work of the alignment task forces. The following template can be used by each task force leader to report on progress and next steps. The summary sheet should be delivered to the project manager at the end of each week.

(Used by each task force to update the project manager
at the end of every week about the team's progress.)

Task force name:

Week ending:

1. Key actions during the past week:

2. Key successes:

3a. Key issues:

3b. Potential solutions/help needed:

4. Next steps/actions:

5. Other key information:

IX. Benchmarking Guidelines and Templates

The following guidelines and templates will help task forces to conduct effective benchmarking (step two of the ten steps listed earlier).

The Basic Steps of Benchmarking

The following basic steps, when followed, will make a benchmarking effort go much more smoothly:

1. Identify the aspects of the influence system that the task force would like to benchmark.
2. Select companies to benchmark.
3. Design a benchmarking interview guide.
4. Contact companies to schedule the interviews.
5. Send the interview guide to the benchmarked company's contacts.
6. Conduct the interview.
7. Summarize the findings.

Benchmarking Dos and Don'ts

Do	Don't
Be organized (preset questions, coordinate interviews between task forces).	Be haphazard.
Look for ideas.	Look for magic solutions.
Understand the differences between companies.	Assume that the information can be compared as "apples to apples."
Conduct telephone interviews, with site visits being extraordinary.	Let benchmarking get too expensive and time-consuming by doing many site visits.
Share information with participating companies.	Just take information and not give any.
Look beyond your company size and industry sector.	Get caught up in your own size and industry.
Ensure confidentiality.	Breech a company's confidentiality.
Look for directional trends and order of magnitude.	Try to get the data too precise.

To ensure effective use of time, a benchmarking interview should be structured and focused. The following sample benchmarking interview guide provides a helpful format for benchmarking discussions.

Sample Benchmarking Interview Guide

Company: _____

Contact Name and Title: _____

Telephone Number: _____

Date of Interview: _____

Interviewers: _____

Selection and Staffing:
- What practices have you put in place to align your recruiting practices with the strategy of the company?
- How are skills, experience, and education requirements determined? By whom?
- How are internal candidates considered for openings in comparison to external candidates?
- What role does line management play in selection and hiring? Human resources?
- What if any training/orientation do new employees receive? How soon after hiring?
- Describe the steps in your selection and hiring process.
- How do you measure the effectiveness of your selection and hiring process?

Succession:
- Do you have a formal succession planning process?
- How far down in the organizational structure does your succession process go?
- What role does line management play in selection and hiring? Human resources?
- Describe the steps in your succession planning process.
- How do you measure the effectiveness of your selection and hiring process?

Any Other Comments:

_____

The following matrix can be used by each task force to summarize the best-practice findings.

Summary of Other Companies' Practices	Companies Applying Practices	Our Company's Current Practices	Future Implications for Our Company	Rationale
1. Individuals are responsible for their own career development	Company A Company B Company C Company X Company Y Company Z	Employees expect managers to be responsible	Communicate the expectation of employee responsibility for their own development, but provide support mechanisms (such as training, counseling from management about career choices, etc.)	• Creates a better match of employee skills and interests with the job
2. Delivery of training by management is an honor	Company B Company C Company Z	Viewed as an imposition on management	Management at all levels measured and rewarded for delivery of training	• Management continues to learn • Sets an example for employees • Employees strive for their chance to become instructors of the future
3. Participation in core company courses is required	Company A Company B Company Y Company Z	No company-wide core courses exist	Establish company core courses required at various points during a person's career (such as new employee)	• Establishes consistency of company training at various points during career development

X. Five Redesign Questions

The members of each alignment task force need to ask themselves the following five key questions when generating redesign recommendations (step three of their ten steps):

1. What can we learn from the feedback the organization gave during the current assessment of this system?
2. What did we find when we detailed the current practices of the influence system?
3. What can we learn from the best-practice companies we talked to?
4. What key enablers are needed to implement our recommendations?
5. How does the redesign impact the other influence systems?

XI. Measurement Guidelines

The following steps will help to ensure the development of focused, effective measures that should be used throughout implementation:

- Have each task force generate a broad list of possible measures for the priority influence system it redesigned.
- Have each task force narrow down its list to no more than two or three key measures (use existing assessment mechanisms and collection tools whenever appropriate) and submit a short list to the core team.
- Have the core team solicit input from management and employees about their reactions to the measurement short list.
- Have the core team refine the short list based on the gathered input.
- Have the core team obtain the advisory team's agreement on the measures.
- Have the task forces and core team establish a baseline of current performance for the agreed-upon measures.
- Have the task forces and core team set preliminary performance targets for each measure.
- Have the core team obtain agreement on the performance targets from the advisory team.
- Have the core team, with the approval of the advisory team, establish accountability mechanisms for the measures, such as incorporating key measures into management and employee performance plans, setting regular measurement reporting processes, and so forth.
- Have the key executives and members of the advisory team communicate the measures to customers and the organization.
- Have the task forces, the core team, and others as identified begin the measurement process when deployment starts, and continue throughout implementation.

- On the basis of the assessment information obtained, have the core team, and others as identified, communicate progress to customers and the organization and make adjustments to the influence systems and/or business strategy as necessary, with the approval of the advisory team.

XII. Detailed Implementation Planning Template

This template can be used by each alignment task force to produce its detailed implementation plans. Using this template will create consistency in format and content between the various task forces' plans.

Task Force: _____

Date: _____

Members: (Leader)

_____

_____

_____

_____

_____

_____

Team Goals/Deliverables:

Description of the goal(s) from the task force charter:

Executive Summary

Task Force Recommendations

Identify the task force's top recommendations in descending priority, along with the main subactions necessary to meet the stated goals and outputs.

Prioritized Recommendations and Key Subactions (Description)	Projected Costs	Expected Benefits (Quantitative/ Qualitative)	Start/End Dates	Responsibility
A.				
B.				
C.				
D.				

Next Steps

Describe in chronological order the next steps that your task force must take to move forward on the implementation effort over the next three to four weeks.

Step	Step Description and Objective	Assigned Responsibility	Target Completion Date	Issues/Comments and Dependencies
1.				
2.				
3.				
4.				
5.				

Detailed Implementation/Rollout Plan

Communication

Complete the following communications strategy matrix for each recommendation, identifying any necessary internal and external announcements to the market, customers, managers, employees, or other stakeholders.

Recommendation A: [for example, to merge office space in order to colocate groups in a particular city]

Stakeholders (Who?)	Objective (Why?)	Message (What?)	Vehicle (How?)	Timing (When?)	Responsibility (Who delivers?)
Executive Management	• Inform of office move • Reasons behind move	• Office consolidation date, reasons • Assignment of offices	• Meeting	Once	COO
All Employees	• Inform of office move • Reasons behind move	• Office consolidation date, reasons • Work space/facilities	• Newsletter • E-mail • Through managers	First few weeks	Division heads
Communities Mayor Local Board Newspapers	• Inform of office move	• New address, phone numbers • New point of contact	• Press release • Advertisement • Letter to mayor	Once	External Communications Department
Customers	• Inform of office move	• New address, phone numbers • New point of contact	• Customer phone calls • Customer letter	First few weeks	Sales and Marketing

Education

Complete the following education plan matrix for each recommendation, identifying objectives, time table, delivery method, and so on that will be needed to achieve implementation.

Recommendation A:

Education Objective	Target Audience	Content/ Delivery	Assigned Responsibility	Timetable/ Duration	Estimated Benefits (Quantity/ Quality)	Projected Costs
1.						
2.						
3.						

Logistics

Each recommendation requires logistical considerations for implementation. In the following table, list the technical, procedural, and/or equipment enablers needed to accomplish the implementation of each recommendation.

Recommendation A:

Need	Requirements for Implementation	Milestones/ Dates	Responsibility/ Comments
Technical			
Procedural			
Equipment			

Tracking and Adjusting

In the following table, describe the method for measuring, monitoring, and adjusting the implementation of the recommendation. This should include the method and frequency of and the responsibility for tracking and adjusting each recommendation.

Recommendation A:

Success Measure(s)	Tracking Method	Tracking Frequency	Adjusting Method	Adjusting Frequency	Responsibility
1.					
2.					
3.					

Conversion Timing

Develop a Gantt chart that identifies the conversion timing of each recommendation for current processes, organizations, responsibilities, systems, and so forth (see following example).

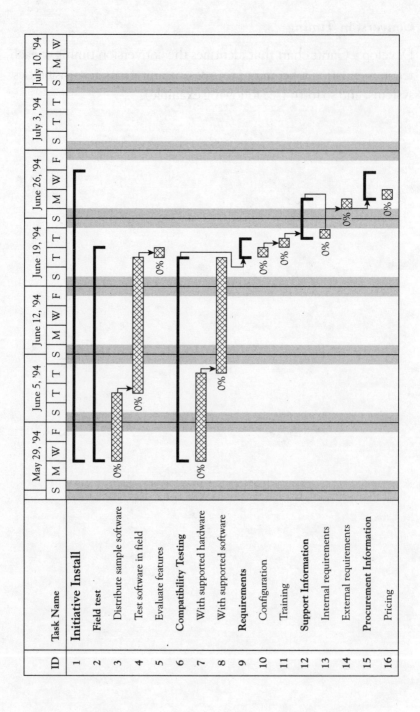

Appendix D

Current Strategy Implementation Research

Study	Focus	Findings
Berg and others (1995)	• The practices required to implement modular production in the apparel manufacturing industry. (Modular production takes a small team a few hours to produce items of clothing, versus several days by other systems.)	• Modular production results in superior quality and productivity. • Implementation of modular production requires training workers in multiskill areas; job rotation; the use of group versus individual incentive pay; pay based on the acquisition of additional skills; and fewer supervisors.
Krafcik and MacDuffie (1995)	• The practices required to implement lean production systems in the auto manufacturing industry. (Lean production utilizes teams of multiskilled employees to produce cars.)	• Lean production uses fewer engineering hours, less inventory space, less employee time, and fewer supplies than mass production systems. • Implementation of lean production requires compensation based on performance, and training of workers in multiskill areas.

Study	Focus	Findings
Huselid (1995)	• Assessed two sets of practices associated with high-performance work environments: employee motivation and employee skills • Surveyed 3,400 firms with more than 100 employees	• Investments in high-performance work practices are related to lower employee turnover, higher productivity, and better company financial performance.
Levine, Lawler, Mohrman, and Ledford (1995)	• The effects of employee involvement (such as self-managed teams and quality circles) on productivity and company financial performance	• Companies that implement employee involvement practices have higher productivity and financial performance than companies that do not. • Involvement practices included rewards for performance (such as gain sharing and profit sharing).
Miller, Lewin, and Lawler (1995)	• Compared company financial performance data with the human resources practices over two years, 1986 and 1987	• Companies with profit-sharing plans and high levels of employee involvement experienced better financial performance and higher productivity levels.
Ichniowski (1990)	• Analyzed the impact of personnel practices on productivity and stock market performance in 200 U.S. manufacturing companies	• Companies with the best performance had high-commitment systems (such as flexible job design, formal training programs, and formal communications systems).

Study	Focus	Findings
		• Companies that had flexible job design but no formal training programs had significantly lower productivity and poorer stock performance. • Organizations must adopt all of the practices of a high-commitment system if they are to experience performance advantages, and training is a critical component.
Arthur (1994)	• The impact of human resources systems on employee turnover in the steel industry	• Companies with human resources systems emphasizing commitment to the company experienced lower turnover rates, less scrap, and higher productivity than systems emphasizing efficiency and reduced labor costs.
Ichniowski, Shaw, and Prennushi (1995)	• Assessed the impact of individual human resources practices and systems of human resources practices on productivity and quality in 30 steel plants (major and smaller producers, with and without unions)	• Individual human resources practices created insignificant changes resulting from incentive pay, teams, and employee/management communication about performance. • Four dominant combinations of human resources practices were identified:

Study	Focus	Findings
		(1) traditional systems, (2) communication systems, (3) high-teamwork systems, and (4) high-performance systems. • The companies with high-performance systems had significantly higher productivity and quality than companies with other systems. • High-performance systems were characterized by extensive job-applicant screening, incentive pay, job assignment flexibility, high employee participation on teams, regular training, and information sharing.
MacDuffie (1995)	• Tested the relationship between human resources practices and performance in 62 automotive assembly plants worldwide	• Identified sets of interrelated practices that create mutually reinforcing support for employee motivation and skill. • Defined three sets of practices that interact to produce high performance: (1) manufacturing, (2) work-systems, and (3) human resources. • Plants using flexible production

Study	Focus	Findings
		systems and high-commitment human resources practices outperformed traditional mass-production systems in both productivity and quality.
Appelbaum and Batt (1994)	• Reviewed 185 case studies and reports on work-reform efforts	• Efforts are most often characterized by varied, piecemeal practices undertaken in an uncoordinated way. • Changes in human resources practices, work organization, quality-management practices, and employee/management relations typically are undertaken separately and exist in parallel, resulting in only moderate changes.

Glossary of Terms

BUSINESS ECOSYSTEM: A system in which companies work cooperatively and competitively to support new products, satisfy customers, and create the next round of innovation in key market segments (Byrne, 1996).

BEHAVIORS: What people regularly say and do to display the competencies they possess.

COALITIONS: Companies working with suppliers, competitors, and/or customers to create new businesses, markets, and industries.

CORE COMPETENCY: A process or collection of skills within a company that establishes customer value, provides competitor differentiation, and is extendable beyond a singular business within a company (Hamel and Prahalad, 1994).

MACROECONOMICS: The assessment of national and/or international economies in terms of whole systems, which takes into account interrelations among sectors of the economy.

ORGANIZATIONAL INFLUENCE SYSTEMS: The management systems and processes within an organization that management can use to bring about the behaviors and competencies needed to achieve a company's business strategy.

REENGINEERING: The fundamental rethinking and redesign of business processes that often creates entirely new processes; combines several processes, functions, or jobs into one process; and results in dramatic improvements in service and/or significant reductions in operating expenses for organizations.

STRATEGY IMPLEMENTATION: The process of taking coordinated actions to realize the goals of a company's business strategy by systematically changing the organizational influence systems to create needed behaviors and competencies of the organization's management and employees.

STRATEGIC INTENT: A tangible corporate goal or destiny that represents a stretch for the organization. It also implies a point of view about the competitive position a company hopes to build over a multiyear span (Byrne, 1996).

STRATEGIC PLANNING: The process of envisioning and designing an organization's future markets, products, and/or services, as well as the necessary competencies, procedures, operations, and systems to achieve that future.

VALUE MIGRATION: The movement of growth and profit opportunities from one industry player to another (Byrne, 1996).

WHITE SPACE: New areas of possible growth that fall between the cracks because they do not naturally match the skills of existing business units (Byrne, 1996).

References

Appelbaum, E., and Batt, R. "The New American Workplace." 1994.

Arthur, J. "Effects of Human Resource Systems on Manufacturing Performance and Turnover." *Academy of Management Journal*, 1994, *37*(3), 670–687.

Auteri, E. "Upward Feedback Leads to Culture Change." *HRMagazine*, June 1994, pp. 78–84.

Berg, P., and others. Preliminary research report presented at the Conference on "What Works at Work," Jan. 1995. Available from The Economic Policy Institute, 1600 L Street NW, Suite 1200, Washington, DC 20036.

Bordogna, J. "Why We Need a National Manufacturing Infrastructure." *Manufacturing Engineering*, Feb. 1996, pp. 136–138.

Bott, K., and Hill, J. "Change Agents Lead the Way." *Personnel Management*, Aug. 1994, pp. 24–27.

Byrne, J. A. "Strategic Planning." *Business Week*, Aug. 1996, pp. 46–52.

Caldwell, B., and Gambon, J. "The Virtual Office Gets Real." *Informationweek*, Jan. 22, 1996, pp. 32–40.

Canna, E. "Nedlloyd's Culture Change." *American Shipper*, June 1995, p. 56.

"Continued Growth—But Big Six Dominate Top Forty." *Consultants News*, Summer 1996, pp. 1, 4.

Chaudron, D. "Frequently Asked Questions About Organizational Change: Answers to Questions Often Asked by Heads of Companies." [http://www.electriciti.com/dchaudron/faq.htm]. 1997.

Creek, R. N. "Organizational Behavior and Safety Management." *Professional Safety*, Oct. 1995, pp. 36–38.

Dahle, C. "Companies Try Before They Buy." *CIO*, Mar. 15, 1996, pp. 14–16.

Dalton, G., and Thompson, P. *Strategies for Career Management*. Provo, Utah: Novations, 1993.

Dobrzynski, J. H. "Yes, He's Revived Sears. But Can He Reinvent It?" *The New York Times*, Jan. 7, 1996, Sec. 3, pp. 1, 8–9.

Du Gay, P., Salaman, G., and Rees, B. "The Conduct of Management and the Management of Conduct: Contemporary Managerial Discourse and the Constitution of the 'Competent Manager.'" *Journal of Management Studies*, May 1996, pp. 263–282.

Dutton, G. "Future Shock: Who Will Run the Company?" *Management Review*, Aug. 1996, pp. 19–23.

Flynn, G. "Cisco Turns the Internet Inside (and) Out." *Personnel Journal*, Oct. 1996, pp. 28–34.

Foster, R. N. *Innovation: The Attacker's Advantage*. New York: Simon and Schuster, 1986.

Franzie, V. "Competencies Emerge in Hiring, Training and Pay." *Personnel Journal*, 1996, *75*(9), 24, 27.

Galpin, T. J. *The Human Side of Change*. San Francisco: Jossey-Bass, 1996.

Galpin, T. J., and Robinson, D. R. "Raising the Bar of Change Management." *Human Resource Professional*, 1997, *10*(2), 15–19.

Gaston, M. "And One Solution: Fishing for the Right Candidate." *Franchising World*, July/Aug. 1996, pp. 19, 21.

Ghemawat, P. "Sustainable Advantage." *Harvard Business Review*, Sept./Oct. 1986, pp. 53–58.

Gephart, M. A. "The Road to High Performance." *Training & Development*, June 1995, pp. 29–38.

Hamel, G., and Prahalad, C. K. *Competing for the Future*. Boston: Harvard Business School Press, 1994.

Hamel, G., and Prahalad, C. K. "Strategy as Stretch and Leverage." *Harvard Business Review*, Mar./Apr. 1993, pp. 75–84.

Harrington, D. "Breaking the Rules." *Editor and Publisher*, July 6, 1996.

Haslett, S. "Broadbanding: A Strategic Tool for Organizational Change." *Compensation & Benefits Review*, Nov./Dec. 1995, pp. 40–46.

Hooper, J. "Borrowing from the Best: How to Benchmark World-Class People Practices." *Human Resource Executive*, June 1992, pp. 38–40.

Huselid, M. "The Impact of Human Resource Management Practices on Turnover, Productivity, and Corporate Financial Performance." *Academy of Management Journal*, 1995, *38*(3), 635–698.

Ichniowski, C. "Human Resource Management Systems and Performance of U.S. Manufacturing Businesses." National Bureau of Economic Research working paper 3449, 1990. Available from National Bureau of Economic Research, 1050 Massachusetts Avenue, Cambridge, MA 02138.

Ichniowski, C., Shaw, K., and Prennushi, G. "The Effects of Human Resource Management Practices on Productivity." In M.A. Gephart, "The Road to High Performance," *Training & Development*, June 1995, p. 34.

Imparato, N., and Harari, O. *Jumping the Curve: Innovation and Strategic Choice in an Age of Transition*. San Francisco: Jossey-Bass, 1994.

Kaplan, R. S., and Norton, D. P. "The Balanced Scorecard: Measures That Drive Performance." *Harvard Business Review*, Jan./Feb. 1992.

Kay, I. "An Interview with Wyatt's Ira Kay." *The Crystal Report*, 1995, *7*(2), 11–14.

Koestenbaum, P. *Leadership: The Inner Side of Greatness*. San Francisco: Jossey-Bass, 1991.

Kotter, J. P., and Heskett, J. L. *Corporate Culture and Performance*. New York: Free Press, 1992.

Krafcik, J., and MacDuffie, J. P. In M. A. Gephart, "The Road to High Performance." *Training & Development*," June 1995, p. 36.

LeBleu, R., and Sobkowiak, R. "New Workforce Competency Models." *Information Systems Management*, Summer 1995, pp. 7–12.

Levine, D. I., Lawler, E., Mohrman, S. A., and Ledford, G. E. "Employee Involvement and Firm Performance." In M. A. Gephart, "The Road to High Performance," *Training & Development*, June 1995, p. 35.

MacDuffie, J. P. "Human Resource Bundles and Manufacturing Performance: Organizational Logic and flexible Production Systems in the World Auto Industry." *Industrial and Labor Relations Review*, Jan. 1995.

Martin, S. L., and Behrens, G. M. "Developing the Next Generation of Executives." *Human Resource Professional*, July/Aug. 1996, pp. 9–13.

McAdams, J. L. *The Reward Plan Advantage: A Manager's Guide to Improving Business Performance Through People*. San Francisco: Jossey-Bass, 1996.

McDowell, C. "Achieving Workforce Competence." *Personnel Journal*, Sept. 1996, pp. 1–10.

McSparran, K., and Edmunds, K. "Changing Culture: Easier Said Than Done." *Beverage World*, Jan. 1996, p. 90.

Miller, D., Lewin, D., and Lawler, E.E. III. "Alternative Pay Systems, Firm Performance, and Productivity." In A. Blinder (ed.), *Paying for Productivity: A Look at the Evidence*. Washington, D.C.: Brookings Institute, 1995.

Mintzberg, H. "The Fall and Rise of Strategic Planning." *Harvard Business Review*, Jan./Feb. 1994, pp. 107–114.

Montgomery, C. A., and Porter, M. E. (eds.). *Strategy: Seeking and Securing Competitive Advantage*. Boston: Harvard Business School Press, 1991.

"More Help Wanted." *Business Week*, Dec. 2, 1996, p. 8.

Mullin, R. "Knowledge Management: A Cultural Evolution." *Journal of Business Strategy*, Sept./Oct. 1996, pp. 56–59.

Nellis, S. K., and Lane, F. "A Second Look at AT&T's Global Business Communications Systems." *Organizational Dynamics*, Spring 1995, pp. 72–76.

Nelson, R. *1001 Ways to Reward Your Employees*. New York: Workman, 1994.

Ohmae, K. *The Mind of the Strategist*. New York: McGraw-Hill, 1982.

Ohmae, K. "Getting Back to Strategy." *Harvard Business Review*, Nov./Dec. 1988, pp. 149–156.

O'Toole, J. *Leading Change*. San Francisco: Jossey-Bass, 1995.

Peak, M. A. "Who's On First?" *HRFocus*, Aug. 1996, p. 24.

People Management Resources. *Action Guide: How to Measure the Impact of Your Company's People Practices*, 1995. Available from People Management Resources, 14780 Osprey Drive, Suite 275, Beaverton, OR 97007

Pitman, B. "How to Build a Learning Culture to Cope with Rapid Change." *Journal of Systems Management*, July 1994, p. 27.

Plishner, E. "Tenneco's New Business." *Journal of Business Strategy*, Nov./Dec. 1996, pp. 14–19.

Porter, M. E. "How Competitive Forces Shape Strategy." *Harvard Business Review*, Mar./Apr. 1979, pp. 137–145.

Porter, M. E. *Competitive Strategy: Techniques for Analyzing Industries and Competitors*. New York: Free Press, 1980.

Porter, M. E. "What Is Strategy?" *Harvard Business Review*, Nov./Dec. 1996, pp. 61–78.

Prahalad, C. K., and Hamel, G. "The Core Competence of the Corporation." *Harvard Business Review*, May/June 1990, pp. 79–91.

Rapaille, G. C. "Changing Culture." *Executive Excellence*, Oct. 1995, pp. 6–7.

Sager, I. "How IBM Became a Growth Company Again." *Business Week*, Dec. 9, 1996, pp. 154–162.

Schmalensee, R. "Do Markets Differ Much?" *American Economic Review*, June 1985, pp. 341–351.

Sherman, S. "A Master Class in Radical Change." *Fortune*, Dec. 13, 1993, pp. 82–90.

Shoesmith, J. "Learning to Love Culture Shock." *Computing Canada*, Feb. 1, 1996, p. 13.

Smart, T. "Jack Welch's Encore." *Business Week*, Oct. 28, 1996, pp. 154–160.

Stewart, T. A. "Managing Change: How to Lead a Corporate Revolution." *Fortune*, Nov. 28, 1994, pp. 48–61.

Wallace, M. J., and Crandall, N. F. "New Deal for Work and Rewards Taking Shape." *American Compensation Association News*, Oct. 1996, pp. 7–8.

Watson Wyatt Worldwide. *Study of the Impact of Organizational Competencies on Company Performance*, 1997. Available from Watson Wyatt Worldwide, 6707 Democracy Boulevard, Suite 800, Bethesda, MD 20817.

Weber, J. "American Standard Wises Up: Smart Manufacturing Methods Make It a Growth Machine." *Business Week*, Nov. 18, 1996, pp. 70–74.

White, J. B. "Reengineering Gurus Take Steps to Remodel Their Stalling Vehicles." *The Wall Street Journal*, Nov. 26, 1996, pp. 1, A13.

Womack, J. P., Jones, D. T., and Roos, D. *The Machine That Changed the World*. New York: Rawson Associates, 1990.

Zack, J. "Ohio's FirstMerit: Sold on a Sales Culture." *American Banker*, Feb. 12, 1996, pp. 4A–5A.

Zamanou, S., and Glasser, S. R. "Moving Toward Participation and Involvement: Managing and Measuring Organizational Culture." *Group & Organization Management*, Dec. 1994, pp. 475–502.

Index

Transaction measurement, 130, 132
Turnover, 215

U

U.S. Department of Transportation, 39

V

Value-based measurements, 130, 132–133
Value migration, 5, 220
Values, change of, 73–74
Virtual offices, 32

W

Wall Street Journal, 6
Wallace, M. J., 27
Wal-Mart, 33
Walsh, M., 28, 30
Watson Wyatt Worldwide, 27, 81
Weber, J., 34–35

Weekly progress summaries, 92, 93, 190, 193
Weiss, W., 28, 30
Welch, J., 10, 19, 26, 28, 30, 31
White, J. B., 6
White space, 5, 11, 220. *See also* Stretch strategy
Willmering, M., 58
Womack, J. P., 35
Work environment, influence systems in. *See* Influence systems; Physical environment
Work-reform efforts, review of, 217

X

Xerox, 97

Z

Zack, J., 28–29, 31
Zamanou, S., 26